Caleb M. Thompson Funeral Records

- *1920's* -

**Depot Street
Shelbyville, Tennessee
Bedford County, TN.**

Compiled By:
Helen Marsh

Book Publishers

**Southern Historical Press, Inc.
Greenville, South Carolina**

SOUTHERN HISTORICAL PRESS, INC.
PO BOX 1267
Greenville, SC   29601

ISBN #978-1-63914-074-9

Printed in the United States of America

FORWARD

This publication contains the Funerial and Burial records from this private business, which are not readily available to the general public. The Caleb M. Thompson Funeral Home is located on Depot Street in Shelbyville, Tennessee. These records were copied and presented here solely for their family and genealogical information that may not be found elsewhere.

ADAMS, BILLIE JEAN
ADAMS, ODELL
ALEXANDER, McKAJA
ALEXANDER, WILLIAM AVERY
ALEXANDER, RUFUS
ALLEN, JOHN HENRY
ALLEY, ALBERT R.
ANDERSON, MRS. TAXANA
ARNOLD, CHARLES SHARP
ARNOLD, FREDONIA
ARNOLD, MRS. CALDONIA V.
ARNOLD, MRS. RENA BRANDON
ARNOLD, SAMUEL B.
ARNOLD, WILLIAM FULTON
ARNOLD, (Infant of Raymond)
BABCOCK, C.W.
BALIFF, WILLIAM RICHARDS
BARTLETT (Infant of Earl)
BASS, WILLIAM ORR
BEARDEN, MRS.VICTORIA
BELL, JAMES LAFAYETTE
BELL, MRS. NANNIE ELIZABETH
BELL, OTIE FLINT
BELL, SHERMAN
BISHOP, IDA RUTH (COL)
BLAKEMORE, EUGENE
BLAKEMORE, MR. ROSS
BLESSING, MISS ELIZABETH
BLIFF, MARY FRANCIS
BOBO, CHANEY V.
BOMAR, CORA
BOMAR, ELNORA (COL)
BOMAR, MRS. LAURA THERESA
BOONE, NATHANIEL F.
BRADSHAW, MRS. R.S.
BRANTLEY, BRUCE K.
BRIDGES, ALBERT EDGAR
BROWN, LEE ODUS
BROWN, MRS. MINNIE NEELY
BROWN, MRS. NANNIE
BRYANT, DR. MARION A.
BRYANT, JOHN C.
BRYMER, EASTER
BRYSON, JOE
BURDETT, MRS. J.R.

BURRELL, MR. CADLE
BURRHAM, MARY RUTH
BURRIS, MRS. REBECCA JANE
BURRIS, ROBERT CECIL
BURROW, WILLIAM ISAC
BURTON (son of Jr.)
BURTON, BEN FRANK
BUTNER, NATHANIEL
CAMPBELL, JAMES ARTHUR
CAMPBELL, MRS. EFFIE NANCE
CANNON, Z. TAYLOR
CAPLEY, JAMES B.
CASTEEL, BESSIE MATDALEEN
CASTEEL, ROY BOON
CHAMBERS, ROBERT NEWTON
CHAPMAN, JAMES SAMUEL
CHUNN, MRS. ELIZA
CLANTON, ANNA LORANE
CLANTON, MRS. EVA GUY
CLARDY, MRS. ANN
CLEMONS, ROBERT P.
CLIFFORD, ADDIE B.
CLIFFORD, JOHN COLEMAN
COBB, MRS. CHLOE
COBLE, THOMAS JACOB, II
COLDWELL, CHARLES
COLEMAN, THOMAS EDWARD
COOK, ALLENE
COOP, JAMES HARVEY
COOPER, MRS. VIRGIE LENTZ
COVINGTON, CHARLES ASKLEN
CRAIG, SAM
CRAWFORD, MAY AGNES
CROSSLIN, ETHEL
CUNNINGHAM, CLARENCE E.
CUNNINGHAM, HUMPHREY D.
CUNNINGHAM, LUCY HAZEL
CUNNINGHAM, MRS. SAMANTHA
CURTIS, ALEXANDER D.
CURTIS, RUTHIE MAY
DAMRON, FRANCIS ESTERLINE
DAMRON, MRS. SARAH MATILDA
DAVIS, JAMES FRANKLIN
DEAN, BILL
DEASON, MRS. ALICE L.

DEERING, JUNE DORRIS
DELK, CLARENCE
DELK, MARY CHRISTINE
DELK, PAULINE
DEMUTH, MRS. BERTHA
DENNIS, JAMES WILLIAM
DENNIS, THOMAS HENRY
DICKENS, MRS. LOMIA CLARK
DRYDEN, MRS. LUCINDA ELLEN
DUNN, ELDRIDGE THORNTON
EASLEY, MRS. IVONIE
ELAM, JAMES A.
ELKINS, ANNIE EULENE
ERVIN, SARAH ANN ELIZABETH
ETHRIDGE, BUD
FALCON, JOSEPH
FARRAR, SAM
FAY, ROBERT EMMET
FISHER, MRS. MARY ADELAIDE
FISHER, MRS. SARAH JANE
FLORIEN, BURTON DUDLEY
FLOYD, MRS. SUSANA MATILDA
FOWLER, ELIZABETH
FRANKLE, ABRAHAM
FREEMAN, WILLIAM
FRIDDLE, ALFRED
FRIDDLE, MRS. NANCY ANN
FUNK, MRS. MATILDA JANE
FUQUA, MRS. ELLA
GAMMILL, MRS. JENNIE
GANT, MRS. TENNIE
GANT, W.W.
GASSAWAY, CHAS. L.
GAZAWAY, THELMA MAY
GENTRY, WILLIAM MORRIS
GILL, MRS. ELORA
GORDON, SAMUEL BALDWIN
GOWAN, ISSOM B.
GREEN, JAMES FRANKLIN
GREEN, JAMES WILLIAM
GREENLEE, JOHN WILLIAMS
GREER, MISS JACKSON
GREER, MISS SALLIE
GREGORY, JOHN THOMAS
GREGORY, PAUL A.

GREGORY, SPENCER GRANGER
GRUBBS, GEO. WILEY
HANON, JOHN D.
HARGIS, MRS. ELLA BLANCHE
HARRIS, SAMUEL RICHARD
HARRISON, MRS. PEARLINA S.
HART, WILLIAM McCLURE
HASTINGS JOE H.
HASTY, MRS. MATILDA
HASTY, RIGGS A.
HAWER, JAMES D.
HAYNES, ANN HOLT
HAYNES, EARNEST THOMAS
HEATH, LEVOY
HELTON, CLARENCE FRANKLE
HELTON, MRS. HETTIE
HELTON, MRS. LELA MAGDALENE
HELTON, MRS. LUCY
HELTON, MRS. MATILDA
HELTON, MRS. NORA ELIZABETH
HICE, ARTHUR J.
HIGH, MARY HOLLAND
HILL, JOHN PAXTON, JR.
HIMES, ED. P.
HIMES, JOHN ALBERT
HIMES, MRS. ADDIE RUTH
HITT, MRS. MARY ELLENDER
HIX, LAWSON G.
HIX, SARAH VIVIAN
HIX, W.W.
HOLDE, FRANCIS ILOE
HOLLIBURTON, CHAS.
HOLT, JOHN EARL
HOLT, WILLIAM EARLE
HORNADAY,(infant of MR. JOE)
HOUSTON, MRS. BLANCHIE V.
HOUSTON, ROBERT WORK
HOWARD, MRS. ROSIE
HOWARD, PAULINE
HOYT, MRS. SALLIE C.
HUDSON, MARY FRANCIS
HUTSON, JAMES L.
INGLE, MRS. VIRGINIA ALICE
IVIE, THOMPSON B.
JENKINS, (Inf of T.C. JONES (COL)

JENKINS, MRS. ANNIE MOORE
JOHNSON, HORACE CLAUDE
JOHNSON, JAMES GILBERT
JOHNSON, SAM HOUSTON
JOHNSTON, FOUNTAIN BASCOM
JONES, DR. SAMUEL ROBERT
JONES, FRANCIS PAUL
JONES, JAMES WILLIAM
JONES, MRS. BERTHA S. NANCE
JONES, MRS. MARY STACY
JONES, WILIAM HARDEN
JORDAN, WILLIAM COLEMAN
KELLY, MRS. SARAH ZANALINE
KENT, ISAAC GARFIELD
KEY, MRS. ETHEL
KIMBRO, DEWEY DEAN
KIMBRO, JAMES ALEXANDER
KIMMONS, JOHN DAVIDSON
KIMMONS, MRS. ANN
KIMMONS, MRS. MARY W.
KIMREY, JAMES ALLEN
KIRKPATRICK, MRS. MATTIE
LACT, MRS. CALLIE FLORENCE
LACY, WALLACE W.
LANDERS, MRS. ANN
LANE, MISS DAISIE
LANGLEY, MRS. SALLLIE E.
LEE (Infant of R.H. Lee)
LENTZ, PARKER
LINDSEY, JAMES
LOKEY, J.W.
LOWE, MRS. MATTIE
LOYD, MRS. EULA B. WAGSTER
LOYD, THELMA CHRISTINE
LUNA, MRS. LUCY
LYNCH, MRS. MARY EVA
McADAMS, GLENN RUSSELL
McANALLY, PAUL
McCONNELL, JOHN SCOTT
McDONALD, MRS. LIZZIE D. JONES
McELROY, SAM
McFADDEN, HENRY CLAY
McFARLAND, MRS. EULA M.
McGILL, JOHN AARON
McGILL, MRS. ELIZABETH

McGILL, RAYMOND INGLE
McGREW, DR. SAMUEL J.
McGREW, JAMES HENRY
McLANE, BESSIE RUTH (COL)
McLANE, FANNY JOHNSON
MARSHALL, L.N.
MARSHALL, MRS. JULIA
MARSHALL, WILLIAM BURR
MARTIN, BASIL, JR.
MARTIN, JAMES D. JR.
MARTIN, MRS. TENNIE
MASSIE, JNO. T.
MAUPIN, JOHN (COL)
MAUPIN, MRS. EMMA SHOFNER
MEACHAM, MRS. MARY M.
MONTGOMERY, ELIAS GREEN
MOONINGHAM, MRS. JENNIE
MOORE, CAL COL
MOORE, EUGENE
MOORE, MATTIE ANN
MOORE, MRS. MARY ETTA
MOORE, MRS. MATTIE TUNE
MORRIS, THOMAS BROWN
MORTON, MANDY
MULLINS, JAMES MADISON
MULLINS, JAMES MARION
MULLINS, MISS MAUDE NORMA
MURDOCK, HIRAM WALACE
NANCE, CLEM (Est.)
NANCE, MRS. MOLLIE
NEAL, MRS. IRENE
NEELY, JESSIE THOMAS
NEELY, MISS ELLIZABETH JANE
NEELY, MRS. JNO. S.
NEIL, JAMES H.
NELSON, JOHN THOMAS
NELSON, MRS. KATE
NEWTON, EARNEST D.
NICHOLSON, YORK P. JR.
NOBLETT, MANNON GORDON
NOBLETT, MRS. ALICE IRENE
NOLEN, MRS. SARAH ANN
O'NEAL, VIRGINIA ARLINE
ODUM, MRS. CORINNE
OLIVER, JAMES

OLLIVER, WILLIAM
PAINTER, JAMES RUFUS
PALMER, MRS. MIGNONETTE
PALMER, WILLIAM EDWIN
PARKER, ELANOR JEAN
PARKER, JOSEPH G., SR.
PARKER, MRS. SARAH ANN
PARKS, MISS LANIA MOORE
PARSON, FRED (COL)
PARSON, MRS. MARY JEAN BUTTS
PARSONS, MRS. SALLIE MOULDER
PARSONS, VOLNEY STRICKLAND
PEACOCK, MRS. SARAH JANE
PHILIPS, MRS. MARY ETTA
PHILLIPS, DONN CARLOS
PHILLIPS, MARVIN MOORE
PHILLIPS, MRS. BERTHA
ELIZABETH
PHILLIPS, SAMJUEL EVERETT
PHILPOT, WILLIAM ALLEN
PHILPOTT, MRS. MARY LOU JANE
PIERCE, MRS. BESSIE NOBLETT
PILKINGTON (Infant of Claude)
PILKINGTON, SIDNEY RUFUS
POARCH, DARATHY SYBLE
POPE, BLANCHIE
POTTS, ALBERT LEE
POTTS, ELISHA H.
POTTS, MARCUS LAFAYETTE
POTTS, ROBERT EARLE
PRICE, LORENZO DENTON
PRICE, MRS. PEARL
PRINCE,(Infant of Clyde Prince)
PRINCE, MARION RHEA
PRINCE, WILLIAM
PROCTOR, MISS ELLA
PROSSER, GROVER HENRY
PROSSER, HOYT
PUCKETT, MRS. MARTHA ANN
RANEY, MRS. WILLIE FLORENCE
RANEY, ROBERT LEE
RANSOM, WILLIAM STREET
REAVIS, GEORGE ROBERT
REED, JAMES GUY
REED, LIFUS OLLIE

REED, MARGARET ELLA MAY
REED, MRS. JANE
REESE, (Infant of Willie G.)
REID, FRANCIS ELOISE
REYNOLDS, THOMAS BENTON
ROBERTSON, MRS. MATTIE B.L.
ROBINSON, ALLIE MARSH
ROBINSON, EVA ELIZABETH
ROBINSON, JAMES MALCOM
ROBINSON, MRS. NETTIE ALMA
ROGERS, MRS. FANNIE LOUISE
ROSBOROUGH, MADISON CLAY
RUCKER, MRS. MALLISIA ANN
RUSS, LEE H.
SAINES CHA RLES CASPER
SAINES, MRS. REBECCA
SANDERS, JAMES ANDERSON
SANDERS, MRS. J.H. (Out of order)
SAVAGE, JAMES WILLIAM
SAVAGE, SUSIE LOU
SCALES, MRS. MOLLIE C.
SCOTT, AFFIE McLANE
SHARP, MRS. PALESTINE
SHEARIN, MRS. ANNIE
SHEARIN, WM. MATTHEW
SHERRILL, PAUL A.
SHOFFNER, MR. JOHN E.
SHOFFNER, MRS. MARY E.
SHOFNER, EDGAR
SHOFNER, JOHN CLAY
SHOFNER, MARY LEONA
SHRIVER, JACK
SHUMARD, MISS LIZZIE
SIMS, JAMES AUSTIN
SIPSEY, MRS. MOLLIE
SMITH, ARHUR EARNEST
SMITH, BESSIE
SMITH, GEORGE C.
SMITH, MRS. GEORGIA A.B.
SMITH, MRS. GEORGIA ROSE
SMITH, PAUL R.
SNELL, LUCIEL JOSEPHINE
SNELL, MRS. MAGGIE A.
SNELL, VERNA A.
SNODDY, MRS. ANNA C.

SORREL, J.E.
SPRINGFIELD, ED
STEPHENS, MRS. ELLEN
STOKES, ED COOPER
STUBBLEFIELD, S. RUSSELL
SULLIVAN, EDWIN
SWING, AUBRY DOUGLAS
TEMPLE, MRS. MARGARET SARAH
THOMAS, JAMES MADISON
THOMPSON, (Infant of J.W.)
THOMPSON, HENRY SAMUEL
THOMPSON, JAMES EDWARD
THOMPSON, JOHN, JR.
THOMPSON, MRS. CYNTHIA
THOMPSON, MRS. EMMA CLARY
THOMPSON, MRS. T. LEIGH
THOMPSON, ROBERT K.
TITTSWORTH, MRS. LUCY
TRACY, GEO. WASHINGTON
TRIBBLE, EARNEST JOE
TRIBBLE, MRS. NANNIE ODLE
TROXLER, JAMES HUFFMAN
TUCKER, MRS. LETTIE BARTLET
TURNER, JAMES FRANKLIN
VANDERGRIFF, MRS. MARY E.
VANN, AVERY LEVOY
VAUGHN, ELISHA
VAUGHN, MRS. CALLIE
VERNON, JAMES McFADDEN
VERNON, MRS. TENNHIE
VICK, MARY ETTA
WALKER, WILLIAM C.
WALLACE, JAMES ANFREW
WALLING, MRS. DELLA EULESS
WARD, JOHN WESLEY
WARNER, MRS. ANNIE ELIZABETH
WARNER, MRS. EMMA R.
WARREN, MRS. ALICE
WARREN, MRS. MINNIE GORE
WATKINS, MRS. PINK
WATSON, CARNEY HOWARD
WELSH, JAMES MARTIN
WHEELER, JOHN DESKIN
WHEELER, MRS. NANNIE
WHEELER, WILLIAM NORRIS

WHITTMORE, JOHN DAVID
WIGGINS, MRS. ANNIE LEE
WILHOIT, MRS. FINETTA
WILHOIT, MRS. MARTHA
WILHOIT, SARAH
WILHOITT, JOHN
WILLIAMS, CHAS. GREGORY
WILLIAMS, JAMES ESTLE
WILLIAMS, JOHN A.
WILLIAMS, MRS. SOPHRONIA
WILLIAMS, MRS. TENNIE DAVIS
WINFORD, JAMES FLOYD
WINSETT, JOHN EARNEST
WISEMAN, MRS. SALLIE
WOMACK, JOHN HARMON
WOMACK, WALTER EMMET
WOOD, WILLIAM (COL)
WOODS, CORNELIA
WHITERSPOON
WOODS, GEORGE ALBERT
WOODS, JAMES ALLEN
WOODS, MRS. FANNIE SANDUSKY'
WOODWARD, GERMON
WOODWARD, JOHN BURTON
WOOSLEY, JNO. MILTON
WOOSLEY, MRS. ELIZABETH
WOOSLEY, MRS. LIZZIE
WORD, MRS. MARTHA J.
WRIGHT, ROBERT SYLVESTER
YANCY, CLAUDE H.
YANCY, MRS. ELLA
YOUNG, GEO. WASHINGTON
YOUNG, MRS. LUA CUMMINGS

ADAMS. BILLIE JEAN
Date of Funeral: Aug 5, 1929   2 p.m.
Casket: Flat Top, size 2/6 & Box $ 12.50
Metal Box Covers   15.00
Date of Death: Aug 4, 1929 at Hurricane Boarding House, Shelbyville, TN
Date of Burial: Aug 5, 1929 Willow Mount cemetery, Shelbyville, TN
Date of Birth: Feb 6, 1929
Age: 0yrs, 5m, 27d.
Color: White
Birthplace: Alabama
Father: Clay Adams
Birthplace: Coffee County, TN
Mother: Willie May Mayse
Birthplace: TN
Physician: Dr. Clinton Brush

ADAMS, ODELL
Date of Funeral: May 26, 1926   10 a.m.
Casket: No. Chatt B., size 5.9 $ 75.00
Date of Death: Mar 25, 1926 at Shelbyville, TN
Place of Funeral: Shelbyville, TN
Interred: Lewisburg, TN
Ordered by Mrs. Sadie Barnes
Date of Birth: Aug 26, 1912
Age: 14 yrs.
Color: White – Occupation: Not Any
Last place of Residence: Shelbyville, TN
Father: Walter Adams
Mother: Bertha Mooningham
Birthplace: ____
Physician: Dr. W.H. Avery

ALEXANDER, McKAJA COOPER
Date of Funeral: Feb 18, 1928   10:30 a.m.
Embalming $ 20.00
Casket: Oct Gray plush, size 6/3   200.00
Burial Garment: suit, Underwear, Sox &
Grave Lining, Metal Box Cover   262.50
Date of Death: Feb 16, 1928 at home, 21st Dist. Bedford County, TN
Place of Funeral: M.E. Church, Shelbyville, TN
Clergyman: Bro. J.M. Cherry
Interred: Willow Mount Cemetery, Shelbyville, TN
Ordered by Children.

ALEXANDER, WILLIAM AVERY
Date of Funeral: Nov 7, 1928   3 p.m.
Casket: Oct, Double Top, size 3/0 $ 33.00
Date of Death: Nov 7, 1828 at 5th District Bedford County, TN
Place of Funeral: Houston Graveyard
Date of Birth: Jul 6, 1827
Age: 1y, 3m, 11d.
Color: White
Birthplace: Bedford County, TN
Father: William R. Alexander
Birthplace: Bedford County, TN
Mother: F.L. Tribble
Birthplace: Bedford County, TN
Physician: Dr. J.P. Temple

ALEXANDER. WILLLIAM RUFUS
Date of Funeral: Jun 24, 1927   2 p.m.
Casket: Sil Gray E. Crape, size 6/3 $ 125.00
Burial Garment: Suit   30.00
Metal Box Covers, Underwear, Ambulance   Total: 163.00
Date of Death: June 24, 1927 at Bedford County Hospital
Place of Funeral: Deason, TN
Clergyman: Dr. S.P. White & Dr. J.E. Vanse
Interred: Houston Graveyard
Date of Birth: Oct 30, 1891
Age: 35y, 7m, 24d.
Color: White – Occupation: Farmer
Married
Birthplace: Bedford County, TN
Father: Robert Alexander
Birthplace: Bedford County, TN
Mother: Margaret Blankenship
Birthplace: Bedford County, TN
Physician: Dr. W.H. Avery

ALLEN, JOHN HENRY
Date of Funeral: Oct 4, 1924   10:30 a.m.
Embalming $ 20.00
Casket: Oct size 6/3   225.00
Burial Garment: Blk. B.C., Shirt   20.00
Metal Covers   No Charge
1 pr. Sox   .50
Shirt, Underware   1.50
Total: $ 267.00
Date of Death: Oct 3, 1924

Place of Funeral: Smiths Chapel
Clergyman: Bro. Demby (Denby)
Interred: Smiths Chapel Cemetery
Date of Death: _____
Age: 76 yrs.
Color: White
Married
Birthplace: ____
Cause of Death: General Ant'otic (?) Infection

ALLEY, ALBERT R.
Date of Funeral: Jun 27, 1926   9 a.m.
Removing Remains: Wartrace to Shelbyville. To P.J. Scudder & to

Cemetery:	$25.00
Drayage to Wartrace Cemetery and Flowers	12.75
Telephone to Nashville Banner	1.85
Funeral Notice in Banner	2.50
Grave Lining	2.00
Total	$44.10

Ordered by J.R. Scudder, Jr.
Date of Death: Jun 23, 1926 at New York City
Place of Funeral: Willow Mount Cemetery, Shelbyville, TN
Clergyman: Dr. J.P. Roberson
Interred: Willow Mount Cemetery, Shelbyville, TN
Date of Birth: ____
Age: 59 yrs.
Birthplace: Bedford County, TN
Father: ____
Mother: ____
No other information.

ANDERSON, MRS. TAXANA

Embalming:	$ 20.00
Casket: E. Crape, size 5/9, & Box	25.00
Hearse, Services, Grave Vault	125.00
Total:	270.00

Ordered by Tom Anderson
Date of Death: Oct 26, 1925 at Shelbyville, TN
Place of Funeral: Shelbyville, TN
Clergyman: Dr. J.P. Robinson
Interred: Willow Mount Cemetery, Shelbyville, TN
Date of Birth Jul 25, 1877
Age: 48 yrs.
Color: White – Occupation: Housewife
Widow

Birthplace: TN
Father: _____ Groomes

ARNOLD, CHARLES SHARP
Date of Funeral: Oct 7, 1929   2 p.m.
Casket: 309 Ash, plush, Full hinge Top, &
Box, Hearse, Services $ 80.00
Burial Garment: Silk Dress, Hose & Gradde and Work   6.45
Metal Box Covers   4.50
Drayage, Grave Lining   1. 50
Chairs, Services   00
Flowers: 12.50
Total: 104.95
Date of Death: Oct 16, 1929 at home in 21st District of Bedford County, TN
Place of Funeral: Home
Clergyman: Rev. W.C. Creasman
Interred: Bedford
Age: 1y, 6m, 24d.
Color: White
Birthplace: Bedford County, TN
Father: Sharp Arnold
Birthplace: Bedford County, TN
Mother: Pauline Ervin
Birthplace: Murray (Maury) County, TN
Physician: Dr. W.H. Avery

ARNOLD, FREDONIA
Date of Funeral: Mar 8, 1925   2 p.m.
Removing Remains from train to Hill Top $ 15.00
Metal Box Covers   5.00
Total: $ 20.00
Date of Death: Mar 6, 1925 at Chattanooga, TN
Place of Burial: Hill Top
Clergyman: Dr. Robinson
Interred: Hill Top, Bedford County, TN
Date of Birth: _____
Age: 76 yrs.
Ordered by: Jno. Himes

ARNOLD, MRS. CALDONIA VICTORIA
Date of Funeral: May 14, 1925   2 p.m.
Casket: Sil. Crape, size 5/9, Box, Hearse, Services $ 125.00
Burial Garment: Dray Dress   20.00
Hose   .50
Total: $ 145.00

Date of Death: May 13, 1925 at 22nd District of Bedford County, TN

Date of Death: May 13, 1925 at 22nd District of Bedford County, TN
Place of Funeral: Home
Clergyman: Jess Hart
Interred: Pleasant Garden Cemetery
Date of Birth: Jun 20, 1869
Age: 56 yrs.
Color: White – Occupation: Housewife
Married
Husband: E.B. Arnold
Physician: Dr. Conditt
Ordered by E.B. ARNOLD

ARNOLD, MRS. RENA BRANDON
Date of Funeral: Nov 29, 1926   2 p.m.
Casket: White, L.S., Chatt, size 6/3 &

Box, Hearse, Service	$ 125.00
Burial Garment: Winding Sheet	15.00
Metal Boards	6.00
Total:	146.00

Date of Death: Nov 27, 1926 at Jno. Brandon's Home, Bedford County, TN
Place of Funeral: Jno. Brandon's home.
Clergyman: Dr. S.P. White
Interred: Willow Mount Cemetery, Shelbyville, TN
Ordered by Arnold & Jno. Brandon
Date of Birth: Feb 20, 1895
Age: 31y, 9m, 7d.
Color: White – Occupation: Housewife
Birthplace: Cannon County, TN
Husband: Vernie Arnold
Father: Jno. Brandon
Birthplace: Cannon County, TN
Mother: Minnie Shelton
Birthplace: Cannon County, TN
Physician: Dr. Jas. L. Morton

ARNOLD, SAMUEL B.
Date of Funeral: Aug 6, 1926   2 p.m.

Embalming	$ 20.00
Casket: ½ Couch, Sil. Gray, size 6/3 &	
Box, Hearse, Services	275.00
Winding Sheet	9.00
Total:	$304.00

Date of Death: Aug 5, 1926 at Home, 6th District of Bedford County, TN
Clergyman: Dr. S.P. White
Interred: Hurricane Grove Cemetery

Date of Birth: Mar 5, 1854
Age: 72 yrs.
Color: White – Occupation: Farmer
Birthplace; Bedford County, TN
Father: Sam Arnold
Birthplace: North Carolina
Mother: Elizabeth Maderis
Birthplace: ____
Physician: Dr. T.J. Coble
Ordered by Family

ARNOLD, WILLIAM FULTON
Date of Funeral: Oct 19, 1929   2:30 p.m.
Embalming: $ 20.00
Casket: Oct White Plush, Hinge Top &
Size 4/6, Box, Hearse, Service   90.00
Burial Garment: Suit, Shirt, Tie, Hose   4.00
Total $125.00
Date of Death: Oct 18, 1929 at Home on Fairfield Pike
Place of Funeral: Northern M.E. Church
Clergyman: Rev. Aiken
Interred: Willow Mount Cemetery, Shelbyville, TN
Ordered by W.C. Arnold

BABCOCK, C.W.
Date of Funeral: (not listed)
Removing Remains Ambulance $ 3.00
Embalming   20.00
Dressing etc: 5.00
Casket: Bronze Finish metal, size 6/3, Hearse   650.00
Services, Clark Vault   125.00
Gents Gray suit   35.00
Underwear, Sox   2.50
Total: $842.50
Ordered by G.E. Babcock
Date of Birth: Dec 6, 1925
Birthplace: 6th District of Bedford County, TN
Place of Funeral: Shelbyville, TN & Hickman County, TN
Date of Birth: Sep 12, 1925
Age: 65yrs.
Color: White – Occupation: Farmer
Birthplace: Missouri
Physician: Dr. W.H. Avery
Cause of Death: Auto Accident

BALIFF, WILLIAM RICHARD
Date of Funeral: Jan 4, 1928   2 p.m.
Casket: Flat Top, Crape, size 6/3. Robe &
Plank, Hearse, Box, Service $ $ 75.00
Date of Death: Jan 4, 1928
Place of Death: Home, Shelbyville Mills
Place of Funeral: Cotton Mills Cemetery
Clergyman: Bro. S.A. Jones
Interred: Cotton Mills Cemetery
Date of Birth: Unknown
Age: 48 yrs.
Color: White – Occupation: Cotton Mills Employee
Married
Birthplace: DeKalb County, TN
Last place of Residence: Shelbyville, TN
Father: Tom Baliff
Birthplace: DeKalb County, TN
Mother: Eliza Winnard
Birthplace: DeKalb County, TN
Physician: Dr. W.H. Avery

BARTLETT, (Son of Earl Bartlett)
Date of Funeral: Dec 25, 1927   2 p.m.
Casket: White, P.K., size 2/0 & Box, metal Covers; $ 29.00
Date of Death: Dec 24, 1927 at 8th District of Moore County, TN
Interred: Waggoner Graveyard
Date of Birth: Oct 24, 1927
Age: 0
Color: White
Birthplace: Moore County, TN
Father: Earle Bartlett
Birthplace: Moore County, TN
Mother: Jane Stone
Birthplace: Bedford County, TN
Physician: Dr. Jno. W. Sutton
Cause of Death: Stillborn

BASS, WILLIAM ORR
Date of Funeral: Jul 25, 1926   3 p.m.
Embalming: $ 20.00
Casket: White P. Oak, size 5/0 &
Box, Hearse, Services   100.00
Metal Box Covers   5.00
Grave Limning   2.00
Total: $125.50

Date of Death: Jul 24, 1926
Place of Death: Bedford County Hospital, Shelbyville, TN
Interred: Willow Mount Cemetery, Shelbyville, TN
Date of Birth: Aug 27, 1917
Age: 9 yrs.
Father: S.D. Bass
Birthplace: TN
Mother: Alice Ruth Kimmons
Birthplace: TN
Physician: Dr. T.J. Coble
Ordered by S.D. Bass

BEARDEN, MRS. VICTORIA
Date of Funeral: Aug 9, 1929   2 p.m.
Embalming: $ 20.00
Casket: Gray State Chatt. 1010, size 6/3   225.00
Hearse, Services, Metal Vault, Style Clark   125.00
Tuc(?)   5.00
Total: 475.00
Ordered by: Cecil Bearden
Date of Death: Aug 8, 1929 at Home, Flat Creek, TN
Clergyman: Rev. Slayden (or Slayton?)
Interred: Flat Creek Cemetery
Date of Birth: Feb 21, 1851
Age: 78y, 5m. 17d.
Color: White – Widow
Birthplace: Bedford County, TN
Husband: W.E. Bearden (divorced)
Father: Wynn Bearden
Birthplace: North Carolina
Mother: Nancy Tribble
Birthplace: Unknown
Physician: Dr. J.T. Conditt

BELL, JAMES LAFAYETTE
Date of Funeral: Oct 5, 1929   10 a.m.
Casket: Oak Gray, size 6/3 &
Box, Hearse, Services $ 145.00
Dressing & etc   5.00
Burial Garment: Suit, Collar, Tie, Shirt   34.00
Metal Box Covers   6.00
Total: $ 190.00
Date of Death: Oct 4, 1929 at Home, Shelbyville, TN
Place of Funeral: Near Beech Grove, TN
Clergyman: Rev. R.H. Haham

Date of Birth: Aug 16, 1849
Age: 80y, 1m, 17d.
Color: White – Occupation: Farmer
Widower
Birthplace: Rutherford County, TN
Last Residence: Shelbyville, TN
Father: Thomas Bell
Birthplace: TN
Mother: Sarah Crosslin
Birthplace: Coffee County, TN
Physician: Dr. T.R. Ray

BELL, MRS. NANNIE ELIZABETH
Date of Funeral: May 15, 1929   2 p.m.
Casket: Sq. Flat Top, Gray Crape &
Box, Metals, Hearse, Services $ 80.00
Date of Death: May 14, 1929 at Bedford County Hospital, Shelbyville, TN
Place of Funeral: Home, Shelbyville Mills
Clergyman: Rev. Kelly
Interred: Cotton Mills
Date of Birth: Jan 11, 1890
Age: 39 y, 4m, 3d.
Color: White – Occupation: Cotton Mill Spinner
Married
Birthplace: Bedford County, TN
Father: Sam Ethridge
Birthplace: Bedford County, TN
Mother: Martha Stewart
Birthplace: Bedford County, TN
Physician: Dr. W.H. Avery

BELL, OTIE FLINT
Date of Funeral: Sep 26, 1928   2 p.m.
Casket: Flat Top, E. Gray, size 6/3 &
Box, Metals, Hearse, Service $ 80.00
Date of Death: Sep 25, 1928 at 7th District of Bedford County, TN
Place of Funeral: Boarding House, Shelbyville, TN
Clergyman: Rev. Frank Trinder (?)
Interred: Center (Cemetery)
Birthplace: Unknown
Age: 39y.
Color: White – Occupation: Mill Operator
Married
Birthplace: Alabama
Last place of Residence: Bedford County, TN

How long of Residence: 1 Month
Father: Henry W. Bell
Birthplace: Alabama
Mother: Sarah Ann Lang (Long?)
Birthplace: Alabama
Physician: Dr. W.H. Avery

BELL, SHERMAN
Date of Funeral: Jul 28, 1925   2:30 p.m.
Casket: Size 6/3, B. Coffin, Box, Man's Robe, Service $ 50.00
Date of Death: Jul 27, 1925
Date of Birth: Jan 26, 1865
Age: 60y.
Color: White – Occupation: Fence Builder
Widower
Last place of Residence: Pleasant Grove, TN
Physician: Dr. Avery

BISHOP, IDA RUTH (COL)
Date of Funeral: Jul 1, 1925
Casket: White L.S., size 2/0, No Box $ 12.50
Date of Death: Jul 1, 1925 at 22nd District of Bedford County, TN
Place of Funeral: Center (Cemetery?)
Age: Stillborn
Father: Henry Bishop
Physician: Dr. Conditt
Ordered by Henry Bishop
(Jim Gambill's Farm)

BLAKEMORE, EUGENE
Date of Funeral: Nov 28, 1925   2:30 p.m.
Embalming $ 200.00
Casket: Blk. B.C. , State, size 6/3, & Hearse, Services   300.00
Case: Cedar   50.00
Grave Lining   2.00
Metal Box Covers   6.00
Drayage & ____?, Service   5.00
Total: $ 382.00
Date of Death: Nov 26, 1925 at Home, Shelbyville, TN
Clergyman: Dr. J.W. Robison
Interred: Willow Mount Cemetery, Shelbyville, TN
Date of Birth: Jul 28, 1852
Age: 73 yrs.
Color: White – Occupation: Retired from Business'
Married

Birthplace: Marshall County, TN
Last place of Residence: Shelbyville, TN
Physician: Dr. Ray

BLAKEMORE, MR. ROSS
Date of Funeral: Dec 10, 1924   11:30 a.m.
Removing Remains from Train to Cemetery $ 10.00
Metal Box Covers: 5.00
Grave Lining   1.50
Drayage & Dirt Cover   1.00
Total: $ 17.50
Date of Death: ____?
Ordered by Eugene Blakemore
Place of Death: Nashville, TN
Charged to Mrs. Ross Blakemore
Interred: Willow Mount Cemetery, Shelbyville, TN
Clergyman: Mr. Boyd
Color: White
Married
Last place of Residence: Nashville, TN

BLESSING, MISS ELIZABETH
Date of Funeral: Feb 1, 1928   2 p.m.
Casket: Sq. Gray rape, size 6/3 &
Box, Hearse, Services, Metal Boards $ 81.00
Date of Death: Jan 31, 1928 at home, Shelbyville, TN
Clergyman: Bro. E.P. Watson
Interred: Coats Grave Yard
Date of Birth: Sep 25, 1852
Age: 7 5y, 4m, 6 d.
Color: White – Occupation: Housewife
Single
Birthplace: Bedford County, TN
Father: Henry Blessing
Birthplace: Bedford County, TN
Mother: Gillie Patterson
Birthplace: Bedford County, TN
Physician: Dr. T.R. Ray

BALIFF, MARY FRANCIS
Date of Funeral: Jan 18, 1929
Casket: Flat Top & Box, size 2/6 $ 20.00
Date of Death: Jan 17, 1929 at Shelbyville, TN
Interred: Shelbyville Mills
Date of Birth: Jan 3, 1929

Color: White
Birthplace: Bedford County, TN
Father: Earnest Baliff
Birthplace: DeKalb County, TN
Mother: Myrtle Lowery
Birthplace: Coffee County, TN
Physician: Dr. W.H. Avery

BOBO, CHANEY V.

Date of Funeral: Sep 20, 1925   2:30 p.m.
Embalming: $ 20.00
Casket: Metal, size 6/6 & Box   650.00
Suit, Collar, Tie   35.00
Metal Box Covers   5.00
Grave Lining   1.50
Total: $711.50
Ordered by Frank Bobo
Date of Death: Sep 19, 1925 at 22nd District of Bedford County, TN
Place of Funeral: Home
Clergyman: Dr. Little
Interred: Flat Creek, TN
Date of Birth: Apr 22, 1853
Age: 75 yrs.
Color: White – Occupation: Farmer
Married
Physician: Dr. Conditt
Cause of Death: Heart Trouble

BOMAR: CORA
Date of Funeral: Sep 20, 1925   2 p.m.
Casket: B, Coffin, Box, size 4/3 & Robe, Services $ 65.00
Date of Death: Sep 19, 1925 at Shelbyville, TN
Place of Burial: Mt. Herman Cemetery
Clergyman: Rev. Hart
Interred: Mt. Herman Cemetery
Date of Birth: Jul 4, 1900
Age: 25 yrs.
Color: White – Occupation: Housewife
Married
Husband: Dave Bomar
Ordered by Dave Bomar and others.

BOMAR, ELNORA (COL)
Date of Funeral: Feb 5, 1925   2 p.m.
Embalming $ 15.00

Casket: Sil Gray, plush, size 6/3	$200.00
Burial Garment: Dress	20.00
Metal Grave Covers	5.00
Total:	$240.00

Place of Death: Shelbyville, TN
Place of Funeral: Shelbyville, TN
Interred: Shelbyville, TN
Date of Birth: ____
Age: 78 yrs.
Color: White
Widow
Birthplace: TN

BOMAR, MRS. LAURA THERESA
Date of Funeral: Apr 10, 1926   9 a.m.
Casket: White P. (illegible), size 6/3 &
Box, Hearse, services, Metal Box Covers $ 150.00
Date of Death: Apr 9, 1926 at Home in Shelbyville, TN
Place of Funeral: Home in Shelbyville, TN
Ordered by Berry Bomar
Clergyman: Dr. S.P. White & Joel E. Vanse
Interred: Willow Mount Cemetery, Shelbyville, TN
Date of Birth: Feb 7, 1876
Age: 49 yrs.
Color: White – Occupation: Housewife
Married
Birthplace: Shelbyville, Bedford County, TN
Father: L.N. Marshall
Birthplace: Coffee County, TN
Mother: Jossie Rankin
Birthplace: Bedford County, TN
Physician: Dr. T.R. Ray

BOONE, NATHANIEL F.
Date of Funeral: Dec 11, 1926*   1:30 p.m.
Removing Remains from Train in Shelbyville to Boonville $ 15.00
Metal Box & Covers   6.00
Total: $ 21.00
Ordered by Frank Wammack
Date of Death: Dec 13, 1926* at Nashville, TN
Place of Burial: Boonville, TN
Clergyman"Dr. Graham
Burial: Dec 14, 1926
Date of Birth: ____
Age: 56 yrs.*

Color: White
Married
Some errors in the dates
No other information

BRADSHAW, MRS. R.S.
Date of Funeral: Mar 5, 1925   4 p.m.
Metal Box Covers $ 5.00
Drayage   1.00
Total: $ 6.00
Ordered by H.A. Bradshaw, Alabama
Date of Death: Mar 3, 1925 at Huntsville, Alabama
No other formation

BRANTLEY, BRUCE K.
Date of Funeral: May 10, 1928   3 p.m.
Casket: Oct E. rape, size 6/3 $ 125.00
Box, Hearse, Metal Box Covers   6.00
Total: $ 131.00
Date of Death: May 9, 1928 at Home, Shelbyville, TN
Place of Funeral: Methodist Church, Shelbyville, TN
Clergyman: Bro. J.W. Cherry
Date of Birth: Oct 18, 1874
Age: 53t, 6m, 20d.
Color: White – Occupation: Barber
Married
Father: W.M. Brantley
Birthplace: Alabama
Mother: Mary Meyers
Birthplace: TN
Physician: Dr. T.R. Ray

BRIDGES, ABERT EDGAR
Date of Funeral: Jun 20, 1926
Casket: White L.S., Flat Top, size 2/0 & Box $ 15.00
Date of Death: Jul 20, 1926 at Hospital, Shelbyville, TN
Place of Burial: New Hermon
Clergyman: ____
Interred: New Hermon
Date of Birth: Jul 19, 1926
Age: 1 day
Color: White
Birthplace: Hospital, Shelbyville, T
Father: A.E. Bridges
Birthplace: TN

Mother: Aliene Noblett Bridges
Birthplace: TN
Physician: Dr. T.J. Coble

BROWN, LEE ODUS
Date of Funeral: Jun 22, 1925   3 p.m.
Removing Remains: Wartrace to Shelbyville and Cemetery $20.00
Grave Lining   1.50
Drayage on Vault, chairs, Cemetery   3.00
Total: $24.50
Ordered by W.A.Brown

BROWN, MRS. MINNIE LEE NEELY
Date of Funeral: Sep 20, 1929   2 p.m.
Embalming: $ 20.00
Casket: State size 6/3 xl   325.00
Hearse, Services, Metal Vault, Style Clark   125.00
Burial Garment: Flesh Silk Dress   32.00
Slippers: 5.00
Grave Lining: 6.00
Drayage, Truck   4.00
Total: $517.00
Date of Death: Sep 19, 1929 at Bedford County Hospital
Place of Funeral: Presbyterian Church, Shelbyville, TN
Clergyman: Dr. Julian & Mr. Mills
Interred: Willow Mount Cemetery, Shelbyville, TN
Date of Birth: Nov 19, 1891
Color: White – Occupation: At home
Married
Birthplace: Bedford County, TN
Husband: Amos Brown
Birthplace: Bedford County, TN
Mother: Mary Wiggins
Birthplace: Bedford County, TN
Physician: Dr. Jas. Morton

BROWN, MRS. NANNIE
Date of Funeral: Dec 7, 1928   1:30 p.m.
Casket: Oct Sil size 6/3, Box, Hearse, Services $ 200.00
Winding Sheet   20.00
Cemetery Service, Grave, Truck, Lining   15.00
Metal Box Covers   5.00
Total $ 240.00
Date of Death: Dec , 1928 at 5th District of Bedford County, TN
Place of Funeral: 5th District of Bedford County, TN

Clergyman: Rev. W.E. Doss
Place of Burial: Houston Graveyard, Bedford County, TN
Date of Birth: Apr 16, 1853
Age: 75y, 7m, 20d.
Color: White – Occupation: Housewife
Widow
Birthplace: Bedford County, TN
Father: Isaac B. Webb
Birthplace: Rutherford County, TN
Mother: Francis Smith
Birthplace: Bedford County, TN
Physician: Dr. W.A. Moon

BRYANT, DR. MARION A.
Date of Funeral: Aug 9, 1928   3 p.m.
2 Trips, From Tullahoma to Shelbyville, TN
Removing remains from Home to Cemetery &
Hearse, Services $ 35.00
Grave Lining   6.00
Metal Box Covers   6.00
Drayage, Tuc(?)   3.00

Total: $ 50.50
Date of Death: Aug 7, 1928 at Ocala, Florida
Place of Funeral: Residence of H.L. Woody. Shelbyville,
Clergyman: Rev. J.W. Cherry
Interred: Willow Mount Cemetery, Shelbyville, TN
Date of Birth: Jan 28, 1875
Age: 53y, 6,. 10d.
Color: White – Occupation: Dr. of Dentistry
Grass Widow
Birthplace: Bedford County, TN
Last place of Residence: Ocala, Fla.

BRYANT, JOHN C.
Date of Funeral: Jul 1, 1929   11 a.m.
Hearse, 2 Trips: Wartrace & Flat reek $ 30.00
Metal Boards   6.00
Grave Lining   2.00

Drayage Services   7.50
Total: $45.50
Date of Death: Jun 29, 1929 at Bessemer, Alabama
Place of Funeral: Christian Church, Flat Creek
Clergyman: Rev. Lewis & Geo. Gowen
Date of Birth: Jul 1, 1929
Interred: Flat Creek Cemetery
Date of Birth: ____
Age: 85 yrs.
Color: White – Occupation: Widower
Birthplace: TN
Last place of Residence: Alabama
Father: Dennis Bryant
Birthplace: TN

BRYMER, EASTER
Date of Funeral: Jul 3, 1929   2 p.m.
Casket: County, size 2/6 $ 6.00
Date of Death: Jul 2, 1929 at home in Shelbyville, TN
Place of Funeral: Home in Shelbyville, TN
Clergyman: Rev. W.E. Doss
Interred: Willow Mount Cemetery, Shelbyville, TN
Date of Birth: Mar 31, 1929
Age: 3m, 2d.
Color: White
Birthplace: Bedford County, TN
Father: Homer Brymer
Birthplace: Coffee County, TN
Mother: Maggie Lowery
Birthplace: Coffee County, TN
Physician: Dr. Jas. L. Morton

BRYSON, JOE

Date of Funeral: Sep 26, 1929   10 a.m.
Casket: No. A, size 6/3, County Coffin $ 12.00
Date of Death: Sep 25, 1020 at Bedford County Hospital
Place of Funeral: Thompson Funeral Home
Interred: Willow Mount Cemetery, Shelbyville, TN
Location of Grave: Pauper
Date of Birth: Unknown
Age: 48 yrs.
Color: White – Occupation: Farmer
Married
Birthplace: Cannon County, TN

Last Residence: Bedford County, TN
Father: Tom Bryson
Birthplace: Cannon County, TN
Mother: Sarah Smith
Birthplace: Cannon County, TN

BURDETT, MRS. J.R.
Date of Funeral: Sep 5, 1929 at Decatur, Alabama   10 a.m.
Also: Shelbyville, TN at 5:30 p.m.
Embalming: $ 25.00
Casket: State Gray Metal, size 6/3 &
Hearse, Services   400.00
Metal Vault, Style: Clark   125.00
Grace Lining, Drayage, Chairs   15.00
Cemetery: 7.50
J.W. Frost   4.50
Total: $565.00
Date of Death: Sep 4, 1929
Place of Funeral: Home, Mrs. Chas. Wiggins, Decatur, Alabama
Interred: Willow Mount Cemetery, Shelbyville, TN
Date: 10y, 4m. 29d. (Dates in error) Probably 50 yrs.
Color: White – Occupation: At Home
Widow
Birthplace: Alabama
Place of residence: Decatur, Alabama
Husband: J.R. Burdett (deceased)
Father: Col. Ben Snodgrass
Birthplace: Alabama
Mother: _____
Birthplace: Alabama
Physician: Dr, Ben L. Burdett

BURRELL, MR. CADLE
Date of Funeral: Aug 9, 1926   2 p.m.
Casket: Sil Gray Ash, plush, size 6/3, Box, Metal Box Covers, Grave Lining,&
Car Driver: $208.00
Date of Death: Aug 8, 1926 at Home, Shelbyville, TN
Place of Funeral: M.E. Church, North

BURRAHAM, MARY RUTH
Date of Funeral: Feb 20, 1925   1 p.m.
Casket: White, plush, size 4.7 &

Metal Covers, Box, Services $ 75.00
Date of Death: Feb 19, 1925 at Shelbyville, TN
Place of Funeral: Mt. Lebanon
Clergyman: Bro. Crouch
Interred: Mt. Lebanon Cemetery
Father: J.E. Burrham
Physician: Dr. Avery
Ordered by J.E. Burrham

BURRELL, MR. CADLE
Date of Funeral: Aug 9, 1926   2 p.m.
Casket: Sil Gray Ash, plush, size 6.3 &
Box, Hearse. Personal Services, Casket, Grave Lining, &
Car Driver: $208.00
Date of Death: Aug 8, 1926 at Home, Shelbyville, TN
Place of Funeral: M.E. Church, North
Clergyman: Dr. Keathley
Interred: Willow Mount Cemetery, Shelbyville, T
Date of Birth: Apr 25, 1839
Age: 87 yrs.
Color: White – Occupation: Carpenter
Married
Birthplace: White County, Illinois
Last place of residence: Shelbyville, TN
Father: David Burrell
Birthplace: New York
Mother: Oachsah Faulkner
Birthplace: ____
Physician: Dr. T.J. Coble

BURRIS, MRS. REBECCA JANE
Date of Funeral: Sep 27, 1927   11 a.m.
Casket: Oct Blk.Crape, size 6/3x, &
Hearse, Box, Service $ 125.00
Burial Garment: Gray Silk Dress   30.00
Grave Lining   3.00
Metal Box Covers   6.00
Total: $ 164.00
Date of Death: Sep 26, 1929 at Home, Shelbyville, TN
Place of Funeral: Home, Shelbyville, TN
Clergyman: Rev. Creasman
Interred: Willow Mount Cemetery, Shelbyville, TN
Date of Birth: ay 16, 1857
Age: 72y, 4m, 10d.
Color: White – Occupation: At Home

Widow
Birthplace: Bedford County, TN
Father: John Pressgrove
Birthplace: Bedford County, TN
Mother: Harriett Haynes
Birthplace: Bedford County, TN
Physician: Dr. W.H. Avery

BURRIS, ROBERT CECIL
Date of Funeral: Jul 21, 1926   11:30 a.m.
Casket: White L.S., Flat Top, size 2/0 & Box $ 15.00
Ordered by Richard Burris
Date of Death: Jul 20, 1926 at Home, Bedford County, TN
Interred: Willow Mount Cemetery, Shelbyville, TN
Date of Birth: Jul 20, 1926
Age: 0
Birthplace: Bedford County, TN
Father: Richard Burris
Birthplace: TN
Mother: Lila Coots Burris
Birthplace: TN
Physician: Dr. Jas. L. Morton

BURTON, (Son of Geo., Jr.)
Date of Funeral: ____
Embalming: $20.00
Ordered by Thos. L. Bobo, Lynchburg, TN
Date of Death: Jul 25, 1925 at Bedford County Hospital
No other information

BURTON, BEN FRANK
Date of Funeral: Jan 15, 1925   1 p.m.
Embalming: $ 20.00
Casket: No. 8260 Blk., B.C.   250.00
Metal Vault: Clark   125.00
Burial Garment: Blk. B.C. Suit   30.00
Slippers: 2.50
Total: 427.50
Ordered by Nat L. Burton
Date of Death: Jan 14, 1925 at 8th District, Bedford County, TN
Place of Funeral: North Fork Church
Interred: Pressgrove Grave Yard
Date of Birth: Feb 14, 1847
Age: 78 yrs.
Color: White – Occupation: Farmer

Married
Birthplace: Bedford County, TN
How long a Residence: 78 yrs.
Charged to: B.F. Burton's Estate

BUTNER, NATHANIEL
Date of Funeral: Jun 26, 1927   10 a.m.
Casket: B., size 6/3
Ordered by Bedford County, TN
Date of Death: Jun 25, 1925 at Home, 6th District, Bedford County, TN
Interred: Hurricane Grove
Date of Birth: Jul 3, 1860
Age: 66y, 11m, 22d.
Color: White – Occupation: Farmer
Widower
Birthplace: Bedford County, TN
Father: Alex Butner
Birthplace: Unknown
Mother: Millie Drew
Birthplace: Unknown
Physician: Not Any
Cause of Death: Found dead in house.

CAMPBELL, JAMES ARTHUR
Date of Funeral: Feb 15, 1926   2 p.m.
Embalming: Fluid Injection $ 5.00
Casket: Oak Blk B C, size 6/3   175.00
Outside Case: Cedar   50.00
Metal Box Covers   5.00
Underwear   2.50
Total: $ 237.50
Place of Death: Feb 14, 1926 at 21st District, Bedford County, TN
Clergyman: Bro. Geo. Gowan
Interred: Willow Mount Cemetery, Shelbyville, TN
Date of Birth: Oct 3, 1859
Age: 67 yrs.
Color: White – Occupation: Farmer
Married
Birthplace: Bedford County, TN
Physician: Dr. T.J. Coble

CAMPBELL, MRS. EFFIE NANCE
Date of Funeral: Sep 12, 1929   2:30 p.m.
Embalming, Dressing etc., &
Casket: State Gray plush, ½ couch, Metals &
Cedar Box, Grave Lining, Hearse, Services $ 300.00
Date of Death: Sep 11, 1929 at Home, 21st District, Bedford County, TN
Place of Funeral: Home, 21st District, Bedford County, TN
Ordered by D.A. Phillips
Interred: Willow Mount Cemetery, Shelbyville, TN
Date of Birth: Feb 5, 1865
Age: 64y, 7m, 6d.
Color: White – Occupation: At Home
Widow
Birthplace: Bedford County, TN
Father: William Nance
Birthplace: Bedford County, TN
Mother: Mattie Sutton
Birthplace: Coffee County, TN
Physician: Dr. T.J. Coble

CANNON, Z. TAYLOR
Date of Funeral: Apr 8, 1928   2 p.m.
Casket: Gray B.C., State, size 6/3 & Box &
Hearse, Services $ 325.00
Burial Garment: Suit   30.00
Metal Box Covers   5.00
Grave Lining   1.50

Total: $361.50
Date of Death: Apr 7, 1826 at 23rd District, Bedford County, TN
Place of Funeral: 23rd District, Bedford County, TN
Ordered by Mike Cannon
Clergyman: Dr. Joel E. Vanse
Interred: Willow Mount Cemetery, Shelbyville, TN
Date of Birth: Nov 16, 1848
Age: 77 yrs.
Color: White -- Occupation: Farmer
Birthplace: Bedford County, TN
Father: Almond Cannon
Birthplace: Bedford County, TN
Mother: Eleanor Powell
Birthplace: Bedford County, TN
Physician: Dr. T.R. Ray

CAPLEY, JAMES B.
Date of Funeral: Oct 24, 1924   2:30 p.m.
Removing Remains from Train $12.50
Metal Grave Cover   5.00
Total: $17.50
Date of Death: Oct 23, 1924 at Nashville, TN
Place of Funeral: Shelbyville, TN
Clergyman: Bro. Cherry
Interred: Willow Mount Cemetery, Shelbyville, TN
Cause of Death: Appalexy
Ordered by John Henry Brantley
Charged to Mrs. Jos. B. Capley

CASTEEL, BESSIE MAYDALEEN
Date of Funeral: Sep 25, 1928   10 a.m.
Casket: Flat Top L S, size 3/0 & Box $ 17.50
Metal Box overs   3.00
Total: $20.50
Date of Death: Sep 24, 1928 at 20th District, Bedford County, TN
Place of Funeral: 20th District, Bedford County, TN
Clergyman: Rev. Geo. Gowen (Gowan?)
Interred: Raby Grave Yard
Date of Birth: Jun 8, 1927
Age: 1y, 3m, 16d.
Color: White
Birthplace: Bedford County, TN
Father: Carroll Casteel
Birthplace: Bedford County, TN
Mother: Fannie L. Morton

Birthplace: Lincoln County, TN
Physician: Dr. Jas. L. Morton

CASTEEL, ROY BOON
Date of Funeral: Apr 22, 1926   2 p.m.
Casket: Coffin, White L.S., size 3/0 &
Box, Metal Covers $ 22.00
Date of Death: Apr 22, 1926 at Home, Bedford County, TN
Place of Funeral: Raby Grave Yard
Clergyman: Rev. Jesse Hart
Interred: Raby Yard
Date of Birth: Jul 4, 1924
Age: ____
Birthplace: Lincoln County, TN
Physician: Dr. Burdett

CHAMBERS, ROBERT NEWTON
Date of Funeral: Mar 28, 1926   2 p.m.
Embalming: $ 20.00
Casket: Sil Gray Plush, size 6/3 &
Box, Hearse, Services   200.00
Metal Box Covers: 5.00
Union Suit, Sox: 2.50
Total: $252.50
Date of Death: Mar 27, 1926 at Shelbyville, TN
Place of Funeral: Shelbyville, TN
Clergyman: Dr. Vanse & Dr. White
Interred: Burns Cemetery
Date of Birth: Sep 10, 1853
Age: 73 yrs.
Color: White – Occupation: Farmer
Single
Birthplace: Bedford County, TN
Father: Harrison Chambers
Birthplace: Bedford County, TN
Mother: Mary De… (illegible)
Birthplace: Bedford County, TN
Physician: Dr. Ray

CHAPMAN, JAMES SAMUEL
Date of Funeral: May 17, 1926   2 p.m.
Embalming: $ 20.00
Casket: Blk. E. rape. Size 6/3 &
Box, Hearse, Services & Robe   90.00
Metal Boards   5.00

Underwear, Sox   1.50
Total: $116.50
Date of Death: May 14, 1926 at 20th District, Bedford County, TN
Interred: Willow Mount Cemetery, Shelbyville, TN
Date of Birth: Mar 14, 1874
Age: 52 yrs.
Color: White – Occupation: - Black Smith
Married
Birthplace: Giles County, TN
Last place of Residence: 20th District, Bedford County, TN
Father: Mark Chapman
Birthplace: Giles County, TN
Mother: Lou Tidwell
Birthplace: Don't Know
Ordered by Jno. Kimmons

CHUNN, MRS. ELIZA
Date of Funeral: Jan 3, 1929   10:30 a.m.
Embalming: $ 20.00
Casket: Oak, ½ couch, Gray, Plush, Size 6/3   275.00
Box, Hearse, Services
Burial Garment: Gray Silk Dress, Hose, Slippers   35.00
Metal Box Covers   xxx
Grave Lining, Drayage, Chairs   xxx
Total: $ 330.00
Date of Death: Jan 1, 1929 at East Side Hospital, Nashville, TN
Place of Funeral: Home, Will E. Chunn, Shelbyville, TN
Clergyman: Rev. W.E. 1929
Interred: Willow Mount Cemetery, Shelbyville, TN
Date of Birth: Jun 23, 1846
Age: 82y, 6m, 8da.
Color: White – Occupation: Housewife
Widow
Birthplace: TN
Last place of Residence: Nashville, TN
Husband: A.L. Chunn
Father: Alfred Mallard
Birthplace: TN
Mother: Sarah Carnes
Birthplace: TN
Physician: Dr. J.O. Ousley

CLANTON, ANNA LORANE
Date of Funeral: Jul 4, 1926
Casket: Flat Top L.S., size 2/0 & Box $ 15.00

Date of Death: Jul 3, 1926 at 8th District, Bedford County, TN

Date of Death: Jul 3, 1926 at 8th District, Bedford County, TN
Place of Funeral: 8th District, Bedford County, TN
Date of Death: Jul 4, 1926
Interred: Burns Cemetery
Date of Birth: May 24, 1926
Age: 1m, 14d.
Color: White
Birthplace: 8th District, Bedford County, TN
Father: Jake Clanton
Physician: Dr. Jas. L. Morton

CLANTON, MRS. EVA GUY
Date of Funeral: Sep 17, 1926
Casket: White L.S., size 6/3 & Box &
Metal Boards, silk Dress, Hearse, Services $ 125.00
Ordered by Jake Clanton
Date of Death: 8th District at Jno. Lamb Home
Place of Burial: Burns Cemetery
Date of Birth: Apr 2, 1903
Age: 23 yrs.
Color: White – Occupation: Housewife
Married
Birthplace: Bedford County, TN
Husband: Jake Clanton
Father: Jno. L. Lamb
Birthplace: TN
Mother: Jannie Stem
Birthplace: TN
Physician: Dr. Jas. L. Morton

CLARDY, MRS. ANN
Date of Funeral: Feb 7, 1927   11 a.m.
Ambulance: $ 2.00
Embalming: 20.00
Casket: Sil Gray, plush, Batesville, size 6/3 & Box   200.00
Hearse, Services, Metal Covers   6.00
Total $228.00
Date of Death: Feb 6, 1927 at Bedford County Hospital
Place of Funeral: North Fork Church
Clergyman: Dr. Kelly
Interred: Pressgrove Grave Yard
Date of Birth: Apr 16, 1852
Age: 74 yrs.
Color: White – Occupation: Housewife
Birthplace: Bedford County, TN

Last place of Residence: Unionville, TN
Husband: Jim Clardy
Father: Nat. O. (D?) Burton
Birthplace: Bedford County, TN
Mother: Arline Rowland
Physician: Dr. W.H. Avery

CLEMONS, ROBERT P.
Date of Funeral: Apr 14, 1927   1 p.m.
Embalming: $ 20.00
Casket: State Steel Gray, B.C., size 6/3 &
Box, Hearse, Services   325.00
Lot in Cemetery & Grave $30.40
Metal Box Covers   6.00
Grave Lining   3.00
Total: $354.00
Date of Death: Apr 12, 1927 at Home on Fairfield Pike
Place of Funeral: Home on Fairfield Pike
Clergyman: Bro. E.P. Watson
Interred: Willow Mount Cemetery, Shelbyville, TN
Ordered by Clemons Bros., Chattanooga, TN
Date of Birth: May 1, 1845
Age: 82y, 11m, 12d.
Color: White – Occupation: Merchant
Married
Birthplace: Rutherford County, TN
Last place of Residence: 6th District, Bedford County, TN
Father: Robert Clemons
Birthplace: Virginia
Mother: Unknown
Birthplace: Unknown
Physician: Dr. T.R. Ray

CLIFFORD, ADDIE B.
Date of Funeral: Jul 22, 1927
Casket: Flat Top, size 2/0 & Box $ 11.00
Date of Death: Jul 22, 1927 at Home, Shelbyville, TN
Interred: Mt. Herman Cemetery
Date of Birth: Jul 21, 1927
Age: 1d.
Color: White
Birthplace: Shelbyville, TN
Father: William Clifford
Birthplace: Bedford County, TN
Mother: Nola Jenkins

Birthplace: White County, TN
Physician: Dr. W.H. Avery

CLIFFORD, JOHN COLEMAN
Date of Funeral: Mar 4, 1927   3 p.m.
Casket: B. Coffin, size 6.3 &
Box, Hearse, Services, Robe, Underwear $ 55.00
Ordered by Jno. W. Clifford
Date of Death: Mar 3, 1927 at Home, Shelbyville, TN
Place of Funeral: Mt. Herman
Clergyman: Bro. Stem
Interred: Mt. Herman Cemetery
Date of Birth: Aug 7, 1908
Age: 18y, 7m.
Color: White
Birthplace: Bedford County, TN
Father: Jno. W. Clifford
Birthplace: Bedford County, TN
Mother: Gertrude Davis
Birthplace: Bedford County, TN
Physician: Dr. W.H. Avery
Cause of Death: Accidental Pistol Shot

COBB, MRS. CLOE
Date of Funeral: Jun 20, 1929   2:30 p.m.
Casket: Oct Gray L.S., size 6/3, &
Box, Hearse, Services $ 125.00
Burial Garment: Gray Dress   20.00
Hose   1.50
Metal Box Covers   6.00
Total: $ 152.50
Flowers   5.00
Date of Death: Jun 20, 1929 at Home, Mr. Brown, 23rd District, Bedford County, TN
Place of Funeral: Singleton
Clergyman: Rev. Stem
Interred: Bedford County, TN
Date of Birth: Nov 16, 1855
Age: 73y, 7m, 4d.
Color: White – Occupation: At Home
Widow
Birthplace: Moore County, TN
Father: James Marr
Birthplace: TN
Mother: Jennie Steelman

Birthplace: North Carolina
Physician: Dr. Conditt

COBLE, THOMAS JACOB II
Date of Funeral: Mar 15, 1927   2 p.m.
Removing Remains from Bell Buckle to Shelbyville, TN $ 15.00
Hearse, Services at Funeral: 15.00
Metal Box Covers   6.00
Grave Lining   3.00
Drayage & Charges   4.00

Total: $ 43.00
Date of Death: Mar 14, 1927 at Home, Humbolt, TN
Place of Funeral: Home of Dr. T.J. Coble, Shelbyville, TN
Clergyman: Dr. Earnest Bryant & Dr. J.W. Cherry
Interred: Willow Mount Cemetery, Shelbyville, TN
Date of Birth: Nov 117, 1904
Age: 23yrs.
Color: White
Single
Birthplace: Shelbyville, TN
Last place of Residence: Humbolt, TN
Father: George Coble
Birthplace: Bedford County, TN
Mother: Henrietta Steel
Birthplace: Bedford County, TN
Ordered by Geo. Coble
Physician: Dr. T.J. Coble & Dr. B.L. Burdett & Others

COLDWELL, CHARLES
Date of Funeral: Oct 20, 1929   7 p.m.
Casket: Oct Gray L.S., size 6/3 &
Box, Hearse, Services $ 125.00
Burial Garment: Suit, Shirt, Collar, Tie   30.00
Metal Box Covers   6.00
Total: $ 161.00
Date of Death: Oct 19, 1929 at 23rd District, Bedford County, TN
Place of Funeral: Church at Raus, TN
Clergyman: Rev. Clyde Gleaves
Interred: Powell Yard
Date of Birth: Jun 4, 1855
Age: 74y, 4m, 15d.
Color: White – Occupation: Farmer
Married
Birthplace: TN

Last place of Residence: Bedford County, TN
Father: Isac Coldwell
Birthplace: Unknown
Mother: Lucy Parcham
Birthplace: Unknown
Physician: Dr. W.H. Avery

COLEMAN, THOMAS EDWARD
Date of Funeral: Dec 1, 1926   1 p.m.
Embalming: $ 20.00
Casket: 1010 Steel Gray, State Chatt., size 6/3 &
Box, Metals, Covers, 1 Hearse, Services   325.00
Date of Death: Nov 29, 1926 at Home, near Flat Creek
Funeral: Home near Flat Creek
Clergyman: Dr. Geo. Gowan
Date of Birth: Dec 1, 926
Interred: Shook Grave Yard
Date of Birth: Oct 18, 1863
Age: 63 yrs.
Color: White – Occupation: Farmer
Single
Birthplace: Bedford County, TN
Father: Jess Coleman
Birthplace: TN
Mother: Jane Floyd
Birthplace: TN
Physician: Dr. J.T. Conditt

COOK, ALLENE
Date of Funeral: Sep 22, 1927   11 a.m.
Casket: White L.S. Coffin, size 3/0 $ 15.00
Box & No Service
Date of Death: Sep 21, 1927 at Home, 18th District, Bedford County, TN
Interred: Mt. Lebanon
Date of Birth: Nov 20, 1925
Age: 1y, 10m, 1d.
Color: White
Birthplace: Bedford County, TN
Father: Jessie Cook
Birthplace: Bedford County, TN
Mother: Ethel Neely
Birthplace: Bedford County, TN
Physician: Dr. W.H. Avery
Ordered by Jessie Cook

COOP, JAMES HARVEY
Date of Funeral: Aug 17, 1927   11 a.m.
Casket: Blk. E. Crape, size 5/9 &
Box, Hearse, Services $ 100.00
Metal Box Covers   6.00
Total: $ 106.00
Date of Death: Aug 16, 1927 at Home, 5th District, Bedford County, TN
Place of Funeral: Cross Roads
Clergyman: Rev. Gleaves
Interred: Cross Roads Cemetery
Date of Birth: Dec 27, 1841
Age: 85y, 7m, 20d.
Color: White – Occupation: Farmer
Birthplace: Bedford County, TN
Ordered by Sam Coop
Father: Horatio Coop
Birthplace: Bedford County, TN
Mother: Susan Alexander
Birthplace: Rutherford County, TN
Physician: Dr. A.E. Fuston

COOPER, MRS. VIRGIE LENTZ
Date of Funeral: Nov 5, 1927   11 a.m.
Casket: ½ Couch, Gray, size 6/3 &
Crome Gray, Box, Hearse, Services &
Metal Box Covers, Silk Dress & Embalming $225.00
Ordered by Archie Cooper
Date of Death: Nov 8, 1927 at Bedford County Hospital
Place of Funeral: Bedford
Clergyman: Dr. S.P. White
Interred: Bedford
Date of Birth: Oct 30, 1895
Age: 32y, 10d
Color: White – Occupation: Housewife
Married
Birthplace: Bedford County, TN
Husband: Archie Cooper
Father: Jim Lentz
Birthplace: Bedford County, TN
Mother: Mary Capley
Birthplace: Bedford County, TN
Physician: Dr. W.H. Avery

COVINGTON, CHARLES ACKLEN
Date of Funeral: Jan 10, 1926   2:30 p.m.

Casket: Gray BC, ½ Couch, size 6/3 Batesville &
Clark Vault, Embalming, Hearse, Services $ 575.00
Ordered by R.O. Covington, Admr., Wanesville, North Carolina
Date of Death: Jan 8, 1926 at Home, Shelbyville, TN
Place of Funeral: Home, Shelbyville, TN
Clergyman: Dr. Robertson & Dr. Cherry
Interred: Shelbyville, TN
Date of Birth: Aug 31, 1859
Age: 67 yrs.
Color: White – Occupation: Traveling Salesman
Widower
Birthplace: Bedford County, TN
Physician: Dr. G.W. Moody

CRAIG, SAM
Date of Funeral: Apr 4, 1928   11 a.m.
Casket: Oak, Blk. E. Crape size 6/3, Metals &
Box, Hearse, Services $ 115.00
Ordered by Sam A. Craig & Bros.
Date of Death: Apr 3, 1928 at 22nd District, Bedford County, TN
Clergyman: Bro. Frank Tinder (?)
Interred: Center (Church Cemetery)
Date of Birth: Oct 3 1846
Age: 81y, 6m.
Color: White – Occupation: Stone Mason
Widower
Birthplace: Unknown
Last place of Residence: Bedford County. TN
Father: Wm. Craig
Birthplace: Unknown
Mother: Unknown
Birthplace: Unknown
Physician: Dr. Conditt

CRAWFORD, MAY AGNES
Date of Funeral: Sep 11, 1927   2:30 p.m.
Embalming $ 20.00
Casket: White plush Oct, size 4/0 &
Box, Metal Covers, Grave Lining, Ambulance &
Hearse, Services   57.00
Total: $ 77.00
Date of Death: Sep 9, 1927 at Bedford County Hospital
Place of Funeral: Home, Shelbyville, TN
Clergyman: Rev. J.W. Cherry & Rev. Chas. Armstrong
Interred: Jenkins Chapel

Date of Birth: Aug 7, 1922
Age: 5y, 1m, 2d.
Color: White
Single
Birthplace: Bedford County, TN
Father: Joe Crawford
Birthplace: Bedford County, TN
Mother: Nina Shofner
Birthplace: Bedford County, TN
Physician: Dr. W.H. Avery
Cause of Death: Automobile Accident

CROSSLIN, ETHEL
Date of Funeral: Nov 20, 1926
Ordered by _____ Wheeler
Casket: Flat Top L.S., size 3/0 & Box $10.00
Date of Death: Nov 19, 1926 at Home, Wartrace Road
Place of Funeral: Home, Wartrace Road
Clergyman: Dr. S.G. White
Interred: Poor House
Date of Birth: Sep 1, 1925
Age: 1y, 2m, 19d.
Color: White
Birthplace: Bell Buckle, TN
Last place of Residence: 7th District, Bedford County, TN
Father: Leslie Freeman Crosslin
Birthplace: TN
Mother: Fanne Driver
Birthplace: Bell Buckle, TN
Physician: Dr. M.L. Connell

CUNNINGHAM, CLARENCE EUGENE
Date of Funeral: Jan 23, 1926   1 p.m.
Embalming, Fluid Injection $ 3.00
Casket: Blk E. Crape, size 6/3 &
Box, Hearse, Services   100.00
Burial Garment: Blk BC Suit   30.00
Metal Box Covers   5.00
Underwear, Sox   2.00
Total: $142.00
Ordered by Mrs. C.E. Cunningham
Place of Death: 7th District, Bedford County, TN
Place of Funeral: Burns Cemetery
Interred: Burns Cemetery
Date of Birth: Jun 12, 1878

Age: 48 yrs.
Color: White – Occupation: Farmer
Married
Birthplace: TN
Father: W.H. Cunningham
Birthplace: TN
Mother: Susan Barber
Birthplace: TN
Physician: Dr. Fuston
Cause of death: Flu

CUNNINGHAM, HUMPHREY DAVIDSON

Date of Funeral: Nov 3, 1927 10 a.m.	
Embalming	$ 20.00
Casket: O. Gray, Crape. Size 6/3x &	
Box, Hearse, Services	125.00
Burial Garments: Shirt, Collar, Tie, Underwear, Sox	5.75
Metal Box Covers	6.00
2 Extra Trips & Hearse	6.00
Drayage & Tuc (?)	3.50
Grave Lining	3.00
Total:	$ 169.25

Cemetery: Bill: $6.50
Date of Death: Nov 2, 1927 at Bryant Hotel, Shelbyville, TN
Place of Funeral: Home, Miss Joe & Jennie Cunningham
Clergyman: Dr. S.P. White

Interred: Willow Mount Cemetery, Shelbyville, TN
Date of Birth: Oct 18, 1874
Age: 53y, 15d.
Color: White – Occupation: Lumber man
Married
Birthplace: Bedford County, TN
Father: Jas. T. Cunningham
Birthplace: Bedford County, TN
Mother: Samantha Harris
Birthplace: Bedford County, TN
Physician: Dr. W.H. Avery

CUNNINGHAM, LUCY HAZEL

Date of Funeral: Aug 2, 1926
Casket: Flat Top, L.S., size 3/6 & Box, Metal Boards $22.50
Date of Death: Aug 1, 1926 at Home, Sylvan Mills
Place of Funeral: Sylvan Mills
Interred: Sylvan Mills Cemetery

Date of Birth: Feb 9, 1924
Age: 1y, 5m.
Color: White
Birthplace: Bedford County, TN
Father: Leslie Cunningham
Birthplace: TN
Mother: Fanell/Fanie(?) Sanders
Birthplace: TN
Physician: Dr. Fuston

CUNNINGHAM, MRS. SAMANTHA
Date of Funeral: Jul 22, 1927   2 p.m.
Embalming $ 20.00
Casket, Sil Gray Plush, size 6/3 & Hearse, Services   200.00
Metal Vault: Clark   125.00
Grave Lining   3.00
Drayage   5.00
Total $ 353.00
Date of Death: Jul 21, 1927 at 20th District, Bedford County, TN

Place of Funeral: 20th District, Bedford County, TN
Clergyman: Dr. Sharp
Interred: Willow Mount Cemetery, Shelbyville, TN
Date of Birth: Sep 27, 1851
Age: 75y, 9m, 24d.
Color: White – Occupation: Housewife
Widow
Birthplace: Bedford County, TN
Husband: Jas. T. Cunningham
Birthplace: TN
Mother: Miss Moyers
Birthplace: TN
Physician: Dr. W.H. Avery

CURTIS, ALEXANDER D.
Date of Funeral: Jan 3, 1929   9:30 a.m.
Box $ 6.50
Metal Box Covers   3.50
Hearse, Grave Lining, Drayage, Chairs, Services   10.00
Total $ 20.00
Date of Death: Jan 2, 1929 at Chattanooga, TN
Clergyman: Rev. Geo. Gowan
Interred: Willow Mount Cemetery, Shelbyville, TN
Date of Birth: Jan 28, 1927
Age: 5y, 11m, 5d.

Color: White
Birthplace: Davidson County, TN
Last place of Residence: Chattanooga, TN
Father: Robert Curtis
Birthplace: Bedford County, TN
Mother: Myrtle Kimmons
Birthplace: Bedford County, TN

CURTIS, RUTHIE MAY
Date of Funeral: Oct 10, 1926   1 p.m.
Casket: Flat Top L.S., size 3/0 &
Box, Metal Boards, to Sylvan ills $ 22,00
Date of Death: Oct 9, 1926 at Shelbyville Mills (Home)
Place of Funeral: Shelbyville Mills
Clergyman: Dr. S.P. White
Interred: Bedford
Date of Birth: Jul 11, 1925
Age: 1 yr.
Color: White
Father: Wilson Curtis
Birthplace: Bedford County, TN
Mother: Annie Ruth Posy Curtis
Physician: Dr. W.H. Avery

DAMRON, FRANCIS ESTERLINE
Date of Funeral: Aug 29, 1926   10 a.m.
Casket: White, Lamb Skin, size 5/6 &
Box, Hearse, Services $ 110.00
Burial Garment: White Silk Dress   9.00
Slippers, Hose, Metal Box Covers   6.00
Total: $ 125.00
Date of Death: Aug 28, 1926 at Home, Shelbyville, TN
Place of Funeral: Home, Shelbyville, TN
Clergyman: Dr. S.P. White
Interred: Willow Mount Cemetery, Shelbyville, TN
Date of Birth: Sep 8, 1914
Age: 11y, 11m
Color: White – Occupation: School Girl
Single
Birthplace: Bedford County, TN
Father: Jno. Damron
Birthplace: TN
Mother: Sallie Bomar
Birthplace: Arkansas
Physician: Dr. W.H. Avery
Ordered by Mrs. Jno. Damron, McMinnville, TN

DAMRON, MRS. SARAH MATILDA
Date of Funeral: Nov 28. 1927   1:30 p.m.
Casket: Oak Gray, E.C., size 5/9 $ 125.00
Burial Garment   35.00
Slipper   5.00
Metal Box Covers   6.00
Total $ 171.00
Date of Death: Nov 27, 1927 at Home, Shelbyville, TN
Place of Funeral: Home, Shelbyville, TN
Clergyman: Bro. Keathley
Interred: Harts Chapel
Date of Birth: Feb 22, 1865
Age: 62y, 9m, 5d.
Color: White – Occupation: Housewife
Widow
Birthplace: TN
Husband: Paris Damron
Father: Ruben Bomar
Birthplace: TN
Mother: Margaret Norvell
Birthplace: TN

Physician: T.J. Coble

DAVIS, JAMES FRANKLIN
Date of Funeral: Jun 3, 1928   3 p.m.
Embalming $ 20.00
Casket: Oct E. Gray Crape, size 6/3x &
Box, Hearse, Services   125.00
Burial Garment: Suit, Collar, Tie, Shirt   30.00
Metal Box Covers   5.00
Total: $180.00
Date of Death: Jun 2, 1928 at Home, Shelbyville, TN
Place of Funeral: Richmond, TN
Clergyman: Bro. E.R. Watson
Interred: Richmond Cemetery
Date of Birth: Dec 11, 1869
Age: 58y, 5m, 22d.
Color: White – Occupation: Folder in Overall Factory
Married
Birthplace: Bedford County, TN
Father: Thomas Davis
Birthplace: TN
Mother: Elizabeth Phillips
Birthplace: Bedford County, TN
Physician: Dr. A.E. Fuston

DEAN, BILL (COL)
Date of Funeral: Dec 30, 1929   2 p.m.
Casket: O, size 6/3 $ 12.00
Date of Death: Dec 30, 1929 at County Farm
Place of Death: County, Farm
Date of Burial: Dec 31, 1929
Interred: County Farm
Date of Birth: Unknown
Age: About 80 yrs.
Color: (Colored)

DEASON, MRS. ALICE
Date of Funeral: Nov 10, 1927   3 p.m.
Casket: Oct Gray, E. Crape, size 6/3 &
Box, Hearse, Services $ 125.00
Burial Garment: Gray Silk Dress   15.00
Metal Box Covers   6.00
Grave Lining   3.00
Total: $ 149.00
Date of Death: Nov 9, 1927 at Home, Shelbyville, TN

Clergyman: Dr. S.P. White
Date of Birth: Mar 11, 1869
Age: 58y, 7m, 29d.
Color: White – Occupation: Housewife
Married
Birthplace: Bedford County, TN
Husband: J.T. Deason
Father: Jos. M. Brown
Birthplace: TN
Mother: Mary Smith
Birthplace: Unknown
Physician: Dr. Jas. L. Morton

DEERING, JUNE DORRIS
Date of Funeral: Sep 17, 1929   10 a.m.
Casket: Oct White L.S., size 2/6 &
Box, Metals, Grave Lining $ 30.00
Date of Death: Sep 16, 1929 at Home of Dixie Williams,
          626 Deery Street, Shelbyville, TN
Place of Funeral: at Home of Dixie Williams, 626 Deery Street, Shelbyville, TN
Clergyman: rev. W.C. Creasman
Interred: Willow Mount Cemetery, Shelbyville, TN
Age: White
Birthplace: Bedford County, TN
Father: Artie Deering
Birthplace: Rutherford County, TN
Mother: Sarah Williams
Birthplace: Bedford County, TN
Physician: Dr. T.R. Ray

DELK, CLARENCE
Date of Funeral: May 19, 1926   9 a.m.
Casket: Flat op L.S., size 2/0 &
Box, Car, Services $20.00
Date of Death: May 18, 1926 at Home, Shelbyville, TN
Place of Funeral: Willow Mount Cemetery, Shelbyville, T
Clergyman: Dr. Robinson
Interred: Willow Mount Cemetery, Shelbyville, TN
Date of Birth: May 17, 1926
Age: 1 Day
Color: White
Birthplace: Shelbyville, TN
Father: Ed Delk
Birthplace: TN
Mother: Lizzie May Patterson

Birthplace: TN
Physician: Dr. ____

DELK, MARY CHRISTINE
Date of Funeral: Aug 24, 1926   3 p.m.
Casket: White L.S., Chatt., size 6/3 &
Box, Metals, Hearse, Services & Slippers $ 105.00
Date of Death: Aug 23, 1926 at Home, 11th District, Bedford County, TN
Clergyman: Dr. Kerney
Date of Burial: Aug 24, 1926
Interred: Center
Date of Birth: Apr 7, 1905
Age: 21 yrs.
Color: White
Single
Birthplace: Bedford County, TN
Father: J.A. Delk
Birthplace: TN
Mother: Hattie May Casteel
Birthplace: Bedford County, TN
Physician: Dr. White

DELK, PAULINE
Date of Funeral: Nov 8, 1924   2 p.m.
Casket: White, P.K., size 6/0 $ 100.00
Metal Grave Covers   5.00
Total: $ 105.00
No other information

DEMUTH, MRS. BERTHA
Date of Funeral: Jan 11, 1929   10:30 a.m.
Removing Remains, Tent, Drayage, Lining, & etc. $xxx.xx
Date of Death: Jan 9, 1929 at Florence, Alabama
Place of Funeral: M.E. Church, Shelbyville, TN
Clergyman: Rev. W.E. Doss
Interred: Willow Mount Cemetery, Shelbyville, TN
Date of Birth: Dec 5, 1874
Age: 54y, 1m, 4d.
Married
Birthplace: Lewisburg, Marshall County, TN
Last place of Residence: Florence, Alabama
Husband: Emile Demuth
Farther: Joe Cregg
Birthplace: TN
Mother: ____

Birthplace: ____
Physician: ____

DENNIS, JAMES WILLIAM
Date of Funeral: Jul 31, 1927   1 p.m.
Casket: Sil Gray plush, size 6/3 &
Box, Hearse, Services $ 200.00
Metal Box Covers   6.00
Total: $ 206.00
Date of Death: Jul 30, 1927 at 17th District, Marshall County, TN
Place of Funeral: Baptist Church, Lewisburg, TN
Clergyman: Bro. Hardison
Date of Burial: Jul 31, 1927
Interred: Lewisburg, TN
Date of Birth: Jun 14, 1853
Age: 71t, 1m, 16d.
Color: White – Occupation: Brick Mason
Widower
Birthplace: Bedford County, TN
Last place of Residence: Marshall County, TN, all life
Father: Robert Dennis
Birthplace: Wilson County, TN
Mother: Jane McCamie
Birthplace: Bedford County, TN
Physician: Dr. T.J. Coble

DENNIS, THOMAS HENRY
Date of Funeral: Aug 30, 1928   11 a.m.
Embalmimg: $ 20.00
Casket: Batesville, ½ couch, Gray, size 6/3 &
Hearse, Services $225.00
Metal Vault, Style: Clark   125.00
Underwear, Sox   1.50
Grave Lining   xxxx
Total: $371.50
Date of Death: Aug 29, 1 927 at Lewisburg, TN
Place of Funeral Lewisburg, TN
Clergyman: Bro. Creasman
Interred: Lewisburg, TN
Date of Birth: Feb 29, 1890
Age: 38y, 6m.
Color: White – Occupation: Painter
Single
Birthplace: Bedford County, TN
Father: J.N. Dennis

Mother: Callie Holland
Birthplace: TN
Physician: Dr. Reed

DICKENS, MRS. LOMIE? (LONNIE) CLARK
Date of Funeral: Oct 15, 1927   2 p.m.
Removing Remains from Nashville &
Casket: Blk E. Crape, size 6/3 &
Hearse, Services, Metal Covers $ 126.00
Date of Death: Oct 14, 1927
Place of Funeral: Central State Hospital
Clergyman: Bro. Chas. Armstrong
Interred: Crowell Chapel Cemetery
Age: 42 yrs.
Color: White – Occupation: Housewife
Married
Husband: E.B. Dickens

DRYDEN, MRS. LUCINDA ELLEN
Date of Funeral: Aug 8, 1926
Embalming: $ 20.00
Casket: Sil, Gray E. Crape, size ___, & Box &
Hearse, Services   125.00
Burial Garment: Gray Dress   20.00
Metal Box Covers   5.00
Total: $ 175.00
Date of Death: Aug 6, 1926 at Home, 18th District, Bedford County, TN
Place of Burial: Mt. Lebanon Cemetery
Date of Birth: Jun 23, 1867
Age: 69y, 1m, 13d.
Color: White – Occupation: Housewife
Married
Birthplace: Bedford County, TN
Husband: W.J. Dryden
Father: Newton Stevenson
Birthplace: TN
Mother: Puss Hannaway
Birthplace: TN
Physician: Dr. J.W. Reed, Bellfast, TN

DUNN, ELDRIDGE THORNTON
Date of Funeral: May 25, 1928   3 p.m.
Casket: No. 13, size 6/3 & Box, Hearse, Services $ 82.00
Date of Death: May 25, 1928 at Home, 8th District, Bedford County, TN

Place of Burial: Crowell Chapel Cemetery
Clergyman: Bro. Dickens
Date of Birth: May 15, 1870
Age: 58y, 10d.
Color: White – Occupation: Farmer
Married
Birthplace: Rutherford County, TN
Last place of Residence: Bedford County, TN
Father: William Dunn
Birthplace: TN
Mother: Rebecca Smotherman
Birthplace: Rutherford County, TN
Physician: Dr. Jas. L. Morton

EASLEY, MRS. IVONIE
Date of Funeral: Jan 7, 1929   11 a.m.
Removing Remains from Train & Cemetery &
Hearse, Services $ 25.00
Grave Lining   6.00
Drayage & etc.   3.50
Total: $ 34.50
Date of Death: Jan 5, 1929 at Bruceton, TN
Place of Funeral: Willow Mount Cemetery, Shelbyville, TN
Clergyman: Rev. W.E. Doss
Interred: Willow Mount Cemetery, Shelbyville, TN
Date of Birth: _____
Age: 38 yrs.
Color: White – Occupation: Housewife
Married
No other information

ELAM, JAMES A.
Date of Funeral: Aug 2, 1927   11:15 a.m.
Removing Remains from Train to Cemetery $ 15.00
Extra Car for Family $3.50
Lining   3.00
Drayage, Tuc(?)   3.00
Cemetery: $8.50
Total: $ 21.00
Date of Death: Jul 31, 1927 at Chattanooga, TN
Place of Burial: Willow Mount Cemetery, Shelbyville, TN
Clergyman: J.W. Cherry & Rufus Farrow
Interred: Willow Mount Cemetery, Shelbyville, TN
Date of Birth: Oct __, 1882
Age: 45 yrs.
Color: White Married
Last place of Residence: Chattanooga, TN

ELKINS, ANNIE EULENE
Date of Funeral: Feb 7, 1928   1.p.m.
Casket: Oct White L.S., size 3/6 & Box, Hearse, Services $ 55.00
Metal Box Covers   4.00
Total: $ 59.00
Date of Death: Feb 6, 1928 at Home of R.E. Elkins
Place of Funeral: Home of R.E. Elkins
Clergyman: Bro. J.W. Cherry
Interred: Willow Mount Cemetery, Shelbyville, TN
Date of Birth: Apr 2, 1925
Age: 2y, 10m, 4d.

Birthplace: St. Augustine, Florida
Place of Residence: Bedford County, TN
Father: W.L. Elkins
Birthplace: Moore County, TN
Mother: Eulene Stroud
Birthplace: TN
Physician: Dr. W.H. Avery
Ordered by R.E. Elkins

ERVIN, SARAH ANN ELIZABETH
Date of Funeral: Jul 31, 1927   4 p.m.
Casket: Sil E. Crape, size 6/3 $ 125.00
Metal Box Covers   6.00
Total: $ 131.00
Date of Death: Jul 30, 1927 at Home, 19th District, Bedford County, TN
Place of Funeral: Church at Bedford
Clergyman: Rev. Claude Lewis
Interred: Bedford Cemetery – 37 Grandchildren, 26 Great Grandchildren
Date of Birth: Nov 18, 1840
Age: 86y, 9m, 12d.
Color: White – Occupation: Housewife
Married
Birthplace: Bedford County, TN
Husband: J.J. Ervin
Father: Sebron Pigg
Birthplace: Virginia
Mother: Martha Beasley
Birthplace: North Carolina
Physician: Dr. T.J. Coble

ETHRIDGE, BUD
Date of Funeral: May 19, 1926   2 p.m.
Casket: Blk., E. Crape, size 5/9 &
Box, Hearse, Services $ 90.00
Metal Box Covers   5.00
Total: $ 95.00
Ordered by: Sam Ethridge, 422 Burell St., Huntsville, Alabama
Date of Death: May 18, 1926 at Sylvan Cotton Mills
Place of Funeral; Home, Cotton Mills
Clergyman: Dr. Joel E.Vanse
Interred: Willow Mount Cemetery, Shelbyville, TN
Date of Birth: ____
Age: ____
Color: White – Occupation: Worker in Mill
Married

Birthplace: TN
Father: Jess Etheridge
Birthplace: TN
Mother: Elizabeth Hill
Birthplace: TN
Physician: Dr. J.L. Morton

FALCON, JOSEPH
Date of Funeral: Dec 23, 1929   11 a.m.
Casket: Oct Gray L.S., size 6/3 &
Box, Hearse, Services $ 125.00
Burial Garment, Suit, Collar, Tie, Shirt   22,50
Metal Box Covers   6.00
Total: $ 153.50
Date of Death: Dec 22, 1929 at Home, 19th District, Bedford County, TN
Place of Funeral: Bethleham
Clergyman: Rev. J.E. Trotter
Date of Birth: Sep 4, 1856
Age: 73y, 3m, 18d.
Color: White – Occupation: Farmer
Married
Birthplace: La.
Last place of Residence: TN
Father: Joseph Falcon
Birthplace: La.
Mother: Unknown
Birthplace: Unknown
Physician: Dr. T.J. Coble

FARRAR, SAM
Date of Funeral: Jul 22, 1928   2:30 p.m.
Embalming: $ 20.00
Casket: Batesville Steel, ½ couch, Gray, size 6/3 &
Hearse, Services   340.00
Metal Vault, Style, Clark   125.00
Underwear & Sox   2.00
Grave Lining   3.00
Total: $490.00
Date of Death: Jul 21, 1928 at Home, Flat Creek, TN
Place of Funeral: Flat reek Cemetery
Clergyman: Rev. Trotter
Interred: Flat Creek Cemetery
Date of Birth: Oct 15, 1857
Age: 70y, 9m, 6d.
Color: White – Occupation: Merchant
Married
Birthplace: Bedford County, TN
Father: Joe Farrar
Birthplace: North Carolina
Mother: Permelia Farrar
Birthplace: North Carolina
Physician: Dr. J.T. Conditt

FAY, ROBERT EMMET
Date of Funeral: May 21, 1928   2 p.m.
Embalming $ 20.00
Casket: ½ ouch, Gray, Plush, size 6/3   275.00
Box, Hearse, Services, Burial Garments, &
Blue Serge Suit, Shirt, Collar, Tie   33.00
Metal Box Covers   6.00
Grave Lining   6.00
Drayage, Tent, Tuc(?)   2.50
Total: $342.50
No Other Information

FISHER, MRS. MARY ADELAIDE
Date of Funeral: Oct 13, 1926   2 p.m.
Casket: Sil Gray, Plush, size 6/3. Oct Nat. CC. &
Box, Hearse, Services $ 200.00
Burial Garment: Silk Dress (White)   32.50
Metal, Box Covers   6.00
Grave Lining   2.00
Total: $ 240.50
Ordered by Mr. Tom Ed Fisher
Date pf Death: Oct 12, 1926   6:30 p.m.
Place of Death: Home, Shelbyville, TN
Place of Funeral: Home, Shelbyville, TN
Date of Birth: Jan 23, 1973
Age: 53 yrs.
Color: White – Occupation: Housewife
Married
Birthplace: Lincoln County, TN
Last place of Residence: Shelbyville, TN
Husband: Tom Ed Fisher
Father: A.A. McEwen
Birthplace: TN
Mother: Maggie Bentley
Birthplace: TN
Physician: Dr. T.J. Coble

FISHER, MRS. SARAH JANE
Date of Funeral: Oct 26, 1928   11 a.m.
Embalming $ 20.00
Casket: Oct Gray, ½ Couch, plush, size 6/3 &
Box, Hearse, Metals, Services   225.00
Burial Garment: Silk Dress   30.00
Total: $275.00
Date of Death: Oct 25, 1928 at 6th District, Home of Roy Thompson

Place of Funeral: Naz. Church, Shelbyville, TN
Clergyman: Bro. Strickland
Interred: Wheeler Grave Yard
Date of Birth: Apr 18, 1852
Age: 76y, 6m, 7d.
Color: White – Occupation: Housewife
Widow
Birthplace: Bedford County, TN
Father: Henry Wheeler
Birthplace: Wilson County, TN
Mother: Louisa Fisher
Birthplace: Wilson County, TN
Physician: Dr. Jas. L. Morton

FLORIEN, BURTON DUDLEY
Date of Funeral: Apr 9, 1926   11 a.m.
Casket: ½ Couch, Gray, Plush, size 6/3 &
Box: Cedar, Metal Boards, Suit $ 300.00
Ordered by J.N. Dunnaway
Date of Death: Apr 7, 1926 at 8th District, Bedford County, TN
Place of Funeral: Murfreesboro, TN
Clergyman: Dr. ____
Interred: Murfreesboro, TN
Date of Birth: Nov 17, 1886
Age: 39 yrs.
Color: White – Occupation: Construction Foreman
Married
Birthplace: Franklin County, Kentucky
Father: Alonzo B. Florien
Birthplace: ____
Mother: Mary Elizabeth Baker
Birthplace: ____
Physician: Dr. A.E. Fuston

FLOYD, MRS. SUSONA MATILDA
Date of Funeral: Sep 15, 1929   5 p.m.
Casket: Blk. Oct E. Crape, size 6/3 &
Box, Hearse, Metals, Ambulance, Services $ 125.00
Date of Death: Sep 14, 1929 at Bedford County Hospital
Place of Funeral: Thompson Funeral Home
Clergyman: Dr. Julian Sibley
Interred: Willow Mount Cemetery, Shelbyville, TN
Date of Birth: ____
Age: 81 yrs.
Color: White – Occupation: At Home

Grass Widow
Birthplace: Bedford County, TN
Father: Robert Rankin
Birthplace: Rutherford County, TN
Mother: Matilda Lynch
Birthplace: Bedford County, TN
Physician: Dr. W.H. Avery

FOWLER, ELIZABETH
Date of Funeral: Mar 31, 1928
Casket: F.T. White, L.S., Size 2/0 & Box $ 15.00
Date of Death: Mar 31, 192 at Shelbyville, TN
Place of Funeral: Wartrace, TN
Clergyman: _____
Interred: Wartrace,
Date of Birth: Mar 29, 1928
Age: 2 days
Color: White
Birthplace: Shelbyville, TN
Father: B.L. Fowler
Birthplace: Davidson County, TN
Mother: Frances Searcy
Physician: Dr. W.H. Avery

FRANKLE, ABRAHAM
Date of Funeral: Mar 29, 1928   2 p.m.
Embalming: $ 20.00

Casket: Chott 1010 State Gray, size 6/3 &
Hearse, Services   325.00
Outside Case: Cedar   35.00
Metal Box Covers   6.00
Grave Lining   3.00
Drayage & (..?..)   2.50
Total: $391.50
Date of Death: Mar 28, 1928 at Home, Shelbyville, TN
Place of Funeral: Home at Shelbyville, TN
Clergyman: Rev. J.W. Cherry
Interred: Willow Mount Cemetery, Shelbyville, TN
Date of Birth: Jun 24, 1849
Age: 80y, 9m, 3d.
Color: White – Occupation: Dry Goods Merchant
Married
Birthplace: Poland

Last place of Residence: Shelbyville, TN
Father: Unknown
Birthplace: Unknown
Mother: Unknown
Birthplace: Unknown
Physician: Dr. T.J. Coble

FREEMAN, WILLIAM
Date of Funeral: Oct 2, 1926   11 a.m.
Casket: B. (County). Size 5/9 $ 12.00
Date of Death: Oct 1, 1926 at Bedford County Hospital
Place of Funeral: Willow Mount Cemetery, Shelbyville, TN
Clergyman: Dr. J.E. Vanse
Interred: Willow Mount Cemetery, Shelbyville, TN
Date of Birth: Nov 20, 1908
Age: 18 yrs.
Color: White
Single
Birthplace: Coffee County, TN
Last place of Residence: Shelbyville, TN
Father: J.C. Freeman
Birthplace: Cannon County, TN
Mother: Lou Driver
Birthplace: Coffee County, TN
Physician: Dr. Ben Burdett

FRIDDLE, ALFRED
Date of Funeral: Dec 1, 1926   1 p.m.
Casket: Sil Gray Plush, size 6/3 &
Box, Hearse, Metals, Service $ 300.00
No Other Information

FRIDDLE, MRS. NANCY ANN
Date of Funeral: Oct 26, 1927   2 p.m.
Casket: Gray Flat Top, E. Crape, size 6/3 &
Box, Metals, Hearse, Services $ 75.00
Date of Death: Oct 25, 1927 at Shelbyville, TN
Place of Funeral: Old Cemetery, Flat Creek, TN
Clergyman: rev. Geo. Gowan
Interred: Old Cemetery, Flat Creek, TN
Date of Birth: Unknown
Age: About 90 yrs.
Color: White – Occupation: Housewife
Widow
Birthplace: Bedford County, TN

Father: Jim Snoddy
Birthplace: Unknown
Mother: Julia Ann Hazlett
Birthplace: Bedford County, TN
Physician: Dr. Jas. L. Morton
Funeral Charges: Mrs. Sue Hobbs, Dora Snoddy, Hoyt Thornsberry, M.J. Thornsberry, Mrs. N.C. Friddle, and Pension Check.

FUNK, MRS. MATILDA JANE
Date of Funeral: Jan 25, 1928 in Chattanooga, TN

Removing Remains from Train to Willow Mount Cemetery	$ 20.00
Metal Box Covers	6.00
Grave Lining	3.00
Total:	$ 29.00

Funeral Notice $4.50 & Cemetery Bill $6.00
Date of Death: Jan 24, 1928 at Chattanooga, TN
Place of Funeral: Chattanooga, TN
Date of Burial: Jan 26,1928
Date of Birth: _____
Age: 71 yrs.
Color: White – Occupation: Housewife
Widow
Birthplace: Unknown
Last place of Residence: Chattanooga, TN
Husband: Ed Funk

FUQUA, MRS. ELLA
Date of Funeral: Oct 10, 1926   2 p.m.

Removing Remains from Nashville to Shelbyville, TN	$ 25.00
Hearse, Services, at Shelbyville, TN	
One Seven Passenger Sedan	25.00
Total:	$ 40.00

Ordered by Mrs. D.G. Stout, 116 Osmun Place, Ghoca, NY
Date of Death: Oct 7, 1926 at Central State Hospital, Nashville. TN
Place of Burial: Willow Mount Cemetery, Shelbyville, TN
Clergyman: Dr. S. White
Interred: Willow Mount Cemetery, Shelbyville, TN
Date of Birth: _____
Age: 65 yrs.
Widow
Husband: Geo. W. Fuqua

GIMMILL, MRS. JENNIE
Date of Funeral: Jul 15, 1926   2 p.m.
Embalming: $ 20.00
Casket: Oct Gray B.C., size 6/3 & Box &
Hearse, Service   225.00
Metal Box Covers   5.00
Grave Lining   2.00
Inc.   1.00
Total: $ 253.00
Ordered by Horace Raby & Jim Parsons
Date of Death: Jul 14, 1926 at Home, Shelbyville, TN
Place of Funeral: Home, Shelbyville, TN
Clergyman: Dr. S.P. White
Interred: Willow Mount Cemetery, Shelbyville, TN
Date of Birth: Jun 9, 1844
Age: 82 yrs.
Color: White -- Occupation: Housewife
Widow
Birthplace: Bedford County, TN
Husband: J.J. Gammill
Father: Sam Morris
Birthplace: Bedford County, TN
Mother: Nancy Massey
Birthplace: North Carolina
Physician: Dr. T.R. Ray

GANT, MRS. TENNIE C.
Date of Funeral: Nov 1, 1925   2 p.m.
Embalming $ 20.00
Casket: Sil Gray B.C., all Metal, size 6/6 &
Hearse, Services   25.00
Metal Vault, Clark   825.00
Grave Lining   3.00
Inc. Express, Drayage & etc   2.00
Total $ 975.00
Ordered by Mrs. Jessie Templeton & W.W. Gant
Date of Death: Oct 31, 1925 at Shelbyville, TN
Place of Funeral: At Home, Shelbyville, TN
Clergyman: Dr. Vanse & Dr. Robinson
Interred: Willow Mount Cemetery, Shelbyville, TN
Date of Birth: Mar 11, 1840
Age: 85 yrs.
Color: White – Occupation: Housewife
Married
Birthplace: Wilson County, TN

Last place of Residence: Shelbyville, TN
Husband: W.W. Gant
Father: ____ Williams
Mother: Martha Edwards Phillips
Physician: Dr. W.H. Avery

GANT. W.W.
Date of Funeral: Apr 5, 1926   2 p.m.
Embalming $ 20.00
Casket: State Gray B.C., size 6/3xy2   350.00
Hearse, Services, Metal Vault, Style, Clark   140.00
Grave Lining   3.50
Total: $513.50
Ordered by Judge Will Gant
Date of Death: Apr 3, 1926 at Home, Shelbyville, TN
Place of Funeral: Home at Shelbyville, TN
Clergyman: Dr. Jones
Interred: Willow Mount, Cemetery, Shelbyville, TN
Date of Birth: Mar 14, 1831
Age: 94 yrs.
Color: White – Occupation: Farmer
Widower
Birthplace: Bedford County, TN
Father: Jno. Gant
Birthplace: ____
Mother: Sarah Ashley
Birthplace: ____
Physician: Dr. W.H. Avery

GASSAWAY, CHAS. L.
Date of Funeral: Apr 5, 1925   2 p.m.
Removing Remains at Hospital, Town & Home $ 10.00
Embalming: 15.00
Casket: Sil E. rape, size 6/3   125.00
Burial Garment: Broad Cloth Robe   15.00
Underwear & Sox   2.00
Metal Box Covers   5.00
Total: $ 172.00
Ordered by J.L. Gassaway
Date of Death: Apr 4, 1925 at Bedford County Hospital
Place of Funeral: Crowells Chapel
Clergyman: Bro. Russell
Interred: Crowells Chapel Cemetery
Date of Birth: Jan 19, 1901
Age: 24 yrs.

Color: White – Occupation: Farmer
Married
Birthplace: Texas
Last place of Residence: Bedford County, TN
Father: J.L. Gassaway
Birthplace: America
Physician: Dr. Avery
Cause of Death: Pistol Shot

GAZAWAY, THELMA MAY
Date of Funeral: ____
Casket: Flat op L.S., size 2/6 & Box $ 20.00
Date of Death: Jan 18, 1929 at Home, Shelbyville Cotton Mills
Place of Funeral: Home, Shelbyville Cotton Mills
Date of Burial: Jan 19, 1929
Date of Birth: Mar 22, 1928
Age: 9m, 27d.
Color: White
Birthplace: Georgia
Father: Bill Gazaway
Birthplace: Georgia
Mother: Mandy Lawson
Birthplace: Georgia
No other information

GENTRY, WILLIAM MORRIS
Date of Funeral: Dec 30, 1924   2 p.m.
Embalming: $ 20.00
Casket: Sil Gray B.C., size 6/3   250.00
Metal Box Covers   5.00
Suit cloths (Adam & Raby)   30.00
Flowers (John W. & Son)   35.00
Total: $340.00
No other information

GILL, MRS. ELNORA
Date of Funeral: May 23, 1928
Casket: 1010 Gray State, size 6/3 &
Hearse, Services $ 325.00
Outside Case, Cedar   35.00
Metal Box Covers   6.00
Grave Lining   6.00
Drayage & Tuc (?) Exp.   8.50
Total: $ 380.50
Ordered by Chas. Gill

Date of Death: May 22, 1928 at Home, 21st District, Bedford County, TN
Place of Funeral: Jenkins Chapel
Clergyman: Rev. Chas. Armstrong
Date of Burial: May 23, 1928 at Jenkins Chapel
Interred: Jenkins Chapel Cemetery
Date of Birth: Feb 4, 1877
Age: 51y, 3m, 18d.
Color: White – Occupation: Housewife
Birthplace: Bedford County, TN
Father: Wm. H. Jennings
Birthplace: Bedford County, TN
Mother: Rebecca Shoffner
Birthplace: Bedford County, TN
Physician: Dr. T.R. Ray

GORDON, SAMUEL BALDWIN
Date of Funeral: Sep 10, 1926   11 a.m.
Embalming: $ 20.00
Casket: Sil Gray B.C. State, size 6/3 &
Calif. Red Wood Box, Hearse, Services   325.00
Burial Garment: 30.00
Metal Box Covers   6.00
Grave Lining   2.00
Total: $383.00
Date of Death: Sep 9, 1926 at Home, 7th District, Bedford County, TN
Clergyman: Dr. Chas. Armstrong
Interred: Willow Mount Cemetery, Shelbyville, TN
Date of Birth: Mar 19, 1855
Age: 71 yrs.
Single
Birthplace: Bedford County, TN
Father: Samuel Baldwin Gordon
Birthplace: TN
Mother: Amelia Euless
Birthplace: TN
Physician: Dr. W.H. Avery

GOWAN, ISSOM B.
Date of Funeral: Apr 23, 1926   1 p.m.
Embalming: $ 20.00
Casket: Steel Gray, E. Crape, size 6/3, &
Box, Hearse, Services   125.00
Burial Garment: suit (Blue Serge)   30.00
Underwear, Sox   2.00
Total: $177.00

Date of Death: Apr 22, 1926 at Bedford County Hospital, Shelbyville, TN
Place of Funeral: Mother's home near County Line, TN
Clergyman: Dr. Geo. Gowan
Interred: County Line, TN
Date of Birth: Jan 20, 1877
Age: 49 yrs.
Color: White – Occupation: Truck Driver
Married
Birthplace: Bedford County, TN
Physician: Dr. T.R. Ray

GREEN, JAMES FRANKLIN

Date of Funeral: May 8, 1926	2 p.m.	
Embalming:		$ 20.00
Casket: Sil Gray, E. Crape, size 6/3		125.00
Burial Garment:		30.00
Metal Box Covers:		5.00
Suit Underwear & Sox		2.50
Total:		$ 182.50

Ordered by James B. Green
Date of Death: May 7, 1926 at Home, 6th District, Bedford County, TN
Place of Funeral: James B. Green Home, Shelbyville. TN
Clergyman: Dr. Joel E. Vanse & Dr. J.W. Cherry
Interred: Willow Mount Cemetery, Shelbyville, TN
Date of Birth: Feb 6, 1886
Age: 40 yrs.
Color: White – Occupation: Farmer
Married
Birthplace: Bedford County, TN
Last place of Residence: Bedford County, TN, for 40 years
Father: James B. Green
Birthplace: TN' Mother: _____
Physician: Not Any
Cause of Death: Self-inflicted pistol wound

GREEN, JAMES WILLIAM

Date of Funeral: May 29, 1925	1 p.m.	
Casket: Gray E. Crape, size 6/2 &		
Box, Services		$ 125.00
Burial Garment: Black B.C. Suit		15.00
Total:		$ 140.00

Ordered by & charges to T.T. Green
Date of Death: May 28, 1925 at 6th District, Bedford County, TN
Place of Funeral: Gregory Grave Yard
Interred: Gregory Grave Yard

Date of Birth: Apr 7, 1884
Age: 41 yrs.
Color: White -- Occupation: Farmer
Grass Widower
Birthplace: Bedford County, TN
Physician: Dr. Morton

GREENLEE, JOHN WILLIAM
Date of Funeral: ____
Removing Remains $ 5.00
Embalming: 20.00
Ordered by Mrs. J.W. Greenlee
Casket: Nat. Metal, size 6/3 & Box, Personal Services   600.00
Burial Garment: Gray Shirt   35.00
Underwear, Sox   2.50
Dressing etc.   5.00
Total: $667.50
Date of Death: Dec 6, 1925 near Shelbyville, TN
Places of Funeral: Kansas City, Missouri
Date of Birth: May 22, 1862
Age: 63 yrs.
Occupation: Retired Business man
Birthplace: Kentucky
Father: William P. Greenlee
Physician: Dr. W.H. Avery
Cause of Death: Automobile Accident

GREER, MISS JACKSON
Date of Funeral: Jan 31, 1927   10:30 a.m.
Removing Remains from Nashville to Shelbyville, TN $ 25.00
Casket: Steel Gray E. Crape, size 6/3 &
Hearse, Services, Box   125.00
Burial Garment: Gray Silk Dress   28.00
Hose   2.00
Grave Lining   2.00
Metal Box Covers   6.00
Total: $188.00
Ordered by Mrs. Robert Fay
Date of Death: Jan 30, 1927 at Central State Hospital
Place of Funeral: Willow Mount Cemetery, Shelbyville, TN
Clergyman: Dr. J.W. Cherry
Interred: Willow Mount Cemetery, Shelbyville, TN
Date of Birth: ____
Age: ____
Color: White -- Occupation: ____

Single
Last place of Residence: Nashville, TN

GREER, MISS SALLLIE
Date of Funeral: Feb 24, 1929   2 p.m.
Casket: Oct Gray, Plush, size 6/3 &
Box, Hearse, Services $ 225.00
Burial Garment: Gray silk Dress   30.00
Hose, Silk   2.00
Metal Box Covers   6.00
Total: $ 266.00
Place of Death: Feb 27, 1929 at Central State Hospital, Nashville, TN
Clergyman: Rev. W.E. Doss
Date of Burial: Feb 24, 1929
Interred: Willow Mount Cemetery, Shelbyville, TN
Date of Birth: Unknown
Age About 64 yrs. – Occupation: Housewife
Single
No other information

GREGORY, JOHN THOMAS
Date of Funeral: Feb 5, 1928   2 p.m.
Embalming: $ 20.00
Casket: Oct Blk., E. rape, size 6/3   10.00
Metal Box Covers   6.00
Garment: Silk Hose   .50
Total: $126.50
Date of Death: Feb 4, 1928 at Home, 8th District, Bedford County, TN
Place of Funeral: Home, 8th District, Bedford County, TN
Clergyman: Rev. Agee
Date of Burial: Feb 5, 1928
Interred: Holden Grave Yard
Date of Birth: Dec 14, 1853
Age: 84y, 2m, 21d.
Color: White – Occupation: Farmer
Widower
Birthplace: Bedford County, TN
Father: Thomas Gregory
Birthplace: Bedford County, TN
Mother: Mahaley Woods
Birthplace: Bedford County, TN
Physician: Dr. Jas. L. Morton

GREGORY, PAUL A
Date of Funeral: ay 11, 1925   2 p.m.
Removal Remains from Train to Wess Armstrong &
To Cemetery $ 12.50
Metal Box & Covers   5.00
Grave Lining   1.50
Drayage, Box, Chairs   1.00
Total: $ 20.00
Ordered by Wesley Armstrong & Charged to N.T. Gregory
Date of Death: Paul Andrew Gregory (no date given)
Place of Death: Springfield, TN
Place of Funeral: Shelbyville, TN
Clergyman: Dr. E.P. Watson
Date of Funeral: ay 11, 1925
Interred: Willow Mount Cemetery, Shelbyville, TN
Date of Birth: Jun 2, 1849
Age: 76 yrs.
Color: White
Widower
Cause of Death: Chronic Nephritis

GREGORY, SPENCER GRANGER
Date of Funeral: Aug 30, 1929   2:30 p.m.
Embalming: $ 20.00
Casket: Oct Gray, L.S., size 6/3 &
Box, Hearse, Services   130.00
Burial Garment: Suit, Shirt, Collar, Tie   30.00
Underwear, Sox   2.00
Metal Box Covers   6.00
Grave Lining   3.00
Drayage & Inc.   2.12
Total: $197.12
Date of Death: Aug 29, 1929
Place of Death: Home, Shelbyville, TN
Place of Funeral: Home, Shelbyville, TN
Clergyman: Rev. H.P. Keathley & Bro. W.E. Doss
Interred: Willow Mount Cemetery, Shelbyville, TN
Date of Birth: Jul 10, 1874
Age: 55y, 1m, 19d.
Color: White – Occupation: Laborer
Married
Birthplace: Bedford County, TN
Father: Jno. T. Gregory
Birthplace: Bedford County, TN

Mother: Mary Whitman
Birthplace: Bedford County, TN
Physician: Dr. Jas. L. Morton

GRUBBS, GEO. WILEY
Date of Funeral: Aug 6, 1926   2 p.m.
Embalming $ 20.00
Casket: B. Coffin, size 6/3 &
Box, Metal Boards, Hearse, Services, Sox, Shirt, Tie   55.00
Total: $ 75.00
Ordered by Mrs. Aggie Stewart
Date of Death: Aug 3, 1926 at Home of Mrs. Maggie Stewart
Place of Funeral: Home of Mrs. Aggie Stewart
Clergyman: Dr. S.A. Jones
Interred: Coats Grave Yard
Date of Birth: Jun 17, 1856
Age: 70 yrs.
Color: White – Occupation: Carpenter
Widower
Birthplace: Bedford County, TN
Father: Jno. C. Grubbs
Birthplace: Don't Know
Mother: Unknown
Birthplace: Don't Know
Physician: Dr. Jas. L. Morton

HANSON, JOHN D.
Date of Funeral: Apr 10, 1929   4 p.m.
Casket: Oct Gray E. Crape, size 5/9 $ 75.00
Service, Hearse   10.00
Outside Case   6.00
Burial Garment: Shirt   1.50
Underwear   1.50
Hose   .50
Collar   .25
Tie   . 50
Metal Box Covers $ 4.75
Total: $ 100.00
Date of Death: Apr 9, 1929 at Bedford County Hospital, Shelbyville TN
Place of Funeral: Presbyterian Church, Shelbyville, TN
Clergyman: Dr. Julian S. Sibley
Burial: Apr 10, 1929
Interred: Willow Mount Cemetery, Shelbyville, TN
Occupation: Book Keeper (Retired)
Date of Birth: Feb 3, 1844
Age: 85 y, 2m, 6d.
Color: White
Married
Birthplace: Denmark
Last place of Residence, Shelbyville, TN, lived about 69 yrs.
Physician: Dr. T.R. Ray

HARGIS, MRS. ELLA BLANCHE
Date of Funeral: Jul 20, 1928   2 p.m.
Embalming $ 20.00
Casket: Oct Gray plush, size 6/3   200.00
Box, Hearse, Services &
Burial Garment: White Silk Dress   33.00
Metal Box Covers   6.00
Total: $259.00
Paid by J.V. Hargis & Miss Clara Hargis
Date of Death: Home, 6th District, Bedford County
Place of Funeral: Home, 6th District, Bedford County, TN
Clergyman: Rev. J.W. Cherry
Interred: Willow Mount Cemetery, Shelbyville, TN
Date of Birth: Sep 8, 1858
Age: 69y, 10m, 21d.
Color: White – Occupation: Housewife
Married
Birthplace: Indiana
Last place of Residence: Bedford County, TN, 16 yrs.

Husband: J.V. Hargis
Father: Jas. Emery
Birthplace: Ohio
Mother: Caroline Apple
Birthplace: Indiana
Physician: Dr. W.H. Avery

HARRIS, SAMUEL RICHARD
Date of Funeral: Aug 19, 1927   11 a.m.
Casket: Oct White, plush, size 2/6 &
Box, Hearse, Services, Metal Covers $ 55.00
Ordered by Grady Harris
Date of Death: Aug 18, 1927 at Home, Shelbyville, TN
Place of Funeral: Home, Shelbyville, TN
Clergyman: Dr. S.P. White
Interred: Houston Grave Yard
Date of Birth: Dec 19, ____
Age: 2y, 8m, 20d.
Color: White
Birthplace: Shelbyville, TN
Father: Grady Harris
Birthplace: Bedford County, TN
Mother: Janie Corbett
Birthplace: Bedford County, TN
Physician: Dr. Jas. L. Morton

HARRISON, MRS. PEARLINA SHOFFNER
Date of Funeral: Oct 30, 1929   1 p.m.
Casket: State B.C. Gray 1010 Chott, size 6/3 &
Hearse, Services, Tuc, Lining $ 300.00
Metal Vault, Style Clerk   125.00
Total: $ 425.00
Date of Death: Oct 29, 1929 at Home, 23rd District, Bedford County, TN
Place of Funeral: Home, 23rd District, Bedford County, TN
Clergyman: Rev. Chas. Armstrong
Interred: Willow Mount Cemetery, Shelbyville, TN
Date of Birth: Oct 7, 1835
Age: 94y, 22d.
Widow
Birthplace: Bedford County, TN
Father: Austin Shoffner
Birthplace: Bedford County, TN
Mother: Rebecca Cook
Birthplace: TN
Physician: Dr. A.L. Yearwood. Fayetteville, TN

HART, WILLIAM McCLURE
Date of Funeral: Jun 30, 1927   2 p.m.
Embalming $ 20.00
Casket: Oct Sil Gray plush, size 6/3   200.00
Hearse, Service, Grave Lining &
Metal Vault, Style Clark   125.00
Burial Garment: Suit   25.00
Total: 370.00
Date of Death: Jun 29, 1927 at Home, 14th District, Rutherford County, TN
Place of Funeral: 14th District, Rutherford County, TN
Interred: Mount Cemetery, Shelbyville, TN
Date of Birth: Sep 28, 1858
Age: 68y, 9m.
Color: White – Occupation: Farmer
Married
Birthplace: Rutherford County, TN
Father: William Hart
Birthplace: North Carolina
Mother: Sarah Madrel(?)
Birthplace: Rutherford County, TN
Physician: B.L. Ousley, Christiana, TN

HASTINGS, JOE H.
Date of Funeral: Sep 30, 1925   2 p.m.
Embalming $ 20.00
Casket: Metalized, size 6/3 & Box &
Hearse, Services   350.00
Metal Box Covers   5.00
Gray Suit   35.00
Total: $ 410.00
Date of Death: Sep 28, 1925 at 23rd District, Bedford County, TN
Date of Birth: Feb 1, 1836
Age: 89 yrs.
Widower
Birthplace: Bedford County, TN
Physician: Dr. Ray

HASTY, MRS. MATILDA
Date of Funeral: Oct 15, 1926   1 p.m.
Casket: Oct Gray L.S., size 6/0 &
Box, Hearse, Service $ 150.00
Burial Garment: White Silk Dress   29.50
Total: $ 179.50
Ordered by E.B. Arnold
Date of Death: Oct 14, 1926 at 22nd District (Home) Bedford County, TN

Place of Funeral: Pleasant Garden
Clergyman: Rev. Jesse Hart
Interred: Pleasant Garden Cemetery
Date of Birth: Feb 4, 1855
Age: 71 yrs.
Color: White – Occupation: Housewife
Widow
Birthplace: Bedford County, TN (all life)
Father: Banks Burrow
Birthplace: Bedford County, TN
Mother: Jamima Casteel
Birthplace: Bedford County, TN
Physician: Dr. Conditt

HASTY, RIGGS A.
Date of Funeral: Jun 23, 1926   10 a.m.
Casket: Gray, Metalized, not State, size 6/3 & Box &
Hearse, Services $ 350.00
Burial Garment: Suit, clothes, Shirt, Tie   30.00
Hose   .75
Metal Box Covers   5.00
Total: $ 385.75
Date of Funeral: Jun 22, 1926 at 23rd District, Bedford County, TN
Place of Funeral: New Hope
Clergyman: Dr. Vanse & Stem
Interred: New Hope Cemetery
Date of Birth: Jan 17, 1862
Age: 64 yrs.
Color: White – Occupation: Farmer
Married
Birthplace: Bedford County, TN (for 64 Yrs)
Father: Joseph Hasty
Birthplace: Virginia
Mother: Mary Lynn
Birthplace: Virginia
Physician: Dr. E. Fuston

HAWER, JAMES D.
Date of Funeral: Dec 22, 1929   2 p.m.
Removing Remains from Bell Buckle to Cemetery $25.00
Metal Box Covers   6.00
Grave Lining   3.00
Drayage, Tent, hairs, etc   5.00
Cemetery: $8.50

Total: $ 39.00
Date of Death: Dec 20, 1929 at Louisville, Kentucky
Place of Funeral: Louisville, Kentucky and Shelbyville, TN
Clergyman: Dr. J.S. Sibley
Date of Birth: Mar 4, 1967
Age: 62y, 9m, 16d.
Color: White – Occupation: Salesman
Married
Birthplace: Indiana
Last place of Residence: Louisville, Kentucky
Father: Jos. K. Hawes
Birthplace: Indiana
Mother: Eleanor Deity
Birthplace: Indiana
Cause of Death: Lobar Pneumonia

HAYES, ANN HOLT
Date of Funeral: Jun 30, 1928   2 p.m.
Embalming: $ 20.00
Casket: Nat, plush couch, size 2/6 &
Hearse, Services, Grave Lining   150.00
Metal Vault, Style Clark 3/6   80.00
Total: $250.00
Ordered by Clarence Haynes
Date of Death: Jun 29, 1928 at Home, Shelbyville, TN
Place of Funeral: Home, Shelbyville, TN
Clergyman: Bro. Frank Tinder & Bro. J.W. Cherry
Interred: Willow Mount Cemetery, Shelbyville, TN
Date of Birth: Jul 18, 1927
Age: 11m, 11d.
Color: White
Birthplace: Shelbyville, TN
Father: Clarence Haynes
Birthplace: Bedford County, TN
Mother: Louise Holt
Birthplace: Davidson County, TN
Physician: Dr. T.J. Coble

HAYNES, EARNEST THOMAS
Date of Funeral: Jan 18, 1926   3 p.m.
Casket: P.K., size 2/0 &
Car, Box, Services $ 25.00
Date of Death: Jan 18, 1926 at Shelbyville, TN
Place of Funeral: Unionville, TN
Interred: Unionville Cemetery

Date of Birth: Jan 18, 1926
Age: 0 yr.
Color: White
Birthplace: Shelbyville, TN
Father: Earnest Haynes
Physician: Dr. W.H. Avery

HEATH, LEVOY
Date of Funeral: Oct 23, 1929   1:30 p.m.
Removing Remains from Depot, Shelbyville, to
Pleasant Garden $ 25.00
Metal Box Covers   6.00
Grave Lining   3.00
Extra Car   5.00
Drayage & Services to Grave   10.00
Total: $ 49.00
Date of Death: Oct 21, 1929 at Birmingham, Alabama
Place of Funeral: Pleasant Garden Cemetery, Bedford County, TN
Clergyman: Rev. Jesse Hart
Date of Burial: Oct 23, 1929
Interred: Pleasant Garden Cemetery
Date of Birth: Aug 12, 1908
Age: 21y, 2m, 11d.
Color: White – Occupation: Lineman
Single
Birthplace: Bedford County, TN
Last place of Residence: Birmingham, Alabama
Father: Chris Heath
Birthplace: TN
Ordered by: Alabama Power Co.

HELTON, CLARENCE FRANKLE
Date of Funeral: Sep 11, 1929   2 p.m.
Casket: Oct White L.S., size 3/0 &
Hearse, Box, Meals, Services $ 45.00
Date of Death: Sep 10, 1929 at Home, Shelbyville, TN
Place of Funeral: Home, Shelbyville Mills, TN
Clergyman: Rev. W.E. Doss
Date of Burial: Sep 11, 1929
Interred: Shelbyville, Mills Cemetery
Date of Birth: Sep 30, 1927
Age: 1y, 11m, 10d.
Color: White
Birthplace: Walker County, Georgia
Last place of Residence: Shelbyville Mills, TN

HELTON, MRS. LUCY
Date of Funeral: Apr 5, 1928   11 a.m.
Casket: Oct Gray E. Crape, size 6/3 &
Box, Hearse, Service $ 125.00
Burial Garment: White Silk Dress   10.00
Metal Box Covers   5.00
Total: $ 140.00
Date of Death: Apr 4, 1928 at Home, Shelbyville, TN
Place of Funeral: Home, Shelbyville, TN
Clergyman: Bro. J.W. Cherry
Date of Burial: Apr 5, 1928
Interred: Zion church, Giles County, TN
Date of Birth: Aug 8, 1894
Age: 33y, 7m, 27d.
Color: White – Occupation: Housewife
Married
Birthplace: Giles County, TN
Last place of Residence: Shelbyville, TN
Husband: Henry Helton
Father: Wm. Holbert
Birthplace: Giles County, TN
Mother: Eliza Guthrie
Birthplace: Georgia
Physician: Dr. W.H. Avery

HELTON, MRS. MATILDA
Date of Funeral: Jan 21, 1925   1 p.m.
Embalming $ 15.00
Casket: Blk. Eng. Crape, size 5/9   90.00
Burial Garment: Ladies Whit Robe   7.00
Metal Box Covers   5.00
Total: $117.00
Ordered by Robert Helton
Date of Death: Jan 19, 1925 at Sylvan Cotton Mills
Place of Funeral: Sylvan Cotton Mills
Clergyman: Dr. White
Date of Burial: Jan 21, 1925
Interred: Bedford Cemetery
Date of Birth: May 25, 1869
Age: 56 yrs.
Color: White – Occupation: Housewife
Widow
Birthplace: Bedford County, TN
Last place of Residence: Sylvan Cotton Mills
Husband: Ben Helton

Father: Robbie Helton
Birthplace: Bedford County, TN
Mother: Rachel Welch
Birthplace: Alabama
Physician: Dr. W.H. Avery

HELTON, MRS. HETTIE
Date of Funeral: Apr 13, 1925   2 p.m.
Casket: Blk. E. Crape, size 6/3, Box $ 100.00
Metal Box Covers   5.00
Black Crepe Dress   25.00
Total: $ 130.00
Ordered by Sol Helton & Brothers and Sisters
Date of Death: Apr 13, 1925 at Sylvan Cotton Mills, Shelbyville, TN
Place of Funeral: Home, Sylvan Cotton Mills, TN
Clergyman: Dr. J.A. Chenault
Date of Burial: Apr 14, 1925
Interred: Bedford Cemetery
Date of Birth: Aug 18, 1847
Age: 78 yrs.
Color: White
Widow
Physician: Dr. J.L. Morton

HELTON, MRS. LELA MAGDELENE
Date of Funeral: May 30, 1927   1 p.m.
Casket: White L.S., size 6/3, Box &
Hearse, Services, Dress, Metals: $ 125.00
Date of Death: May 29, 1927 at Home, Shelbyville Mills
Place of Funeral: Home, Shelbyville, Mills
Clergyman: Dr. E.P. Watson
Date of Burial: May 30, 1927
Interred: Bedford Cemetery
Date of Birth: Dec 25, 1886
Age: 40y, 4m, 29d.
Color: White – Occupation: Housewife
Married
Birthplace: Rutherford County, TN
Last place of Residence: Shelbyville Mills, TN
Husband: Sol Helton
Father: Robert S. Odell
Birthplace: Rutherford County, TN
Mother: Unknown
Physician: Dr. W.H. Avery

HELTON, NORA ELIZABETH
Date of Funeral: Aug 29, 1926   4 p.m.
Casket: White L.S. Chatt., size 6/3 &
Box, Hearse, Services $ 125.00
Burial Garment: Silk Dress, Slippers, Hose   30.00
Metal Box Covers   6.00
Grave Lining   2.00
Total: $ 163.00
Date of Death: Aug 28, 1926 at Home, Shelbyville, TN
Place of Funeral: Hone, Shelbyville, TN
Clergyman: Dr. J.W. Cherry
Date of Birth: Jam 21, 182
Age: 44 yrs.
Color: White – Occupation: Housewife
Married
Birthplace: Marshall County, TN
Last place of Residence: Shelbyville, TN
Husband: J.W. Helton
Father: Mancell Gregg
Birthplace: Don't know
Mother: Sarah Nolen
Birthplace: Don't know
Physician: Dr. Fuston

HICE, ARTHUR J.
Date of Funeral: Dec 6, 1926
Removing Remains from Hospital (Ambulance) &
Embalming $ 25.00
Burial Garment: Suit   18.00
Underwear & Sox   2.50
Hearse to County Line   10.00
Total: $ 55.50
Ordered by Thomas L. Bobo and charged to T.L. Bobo, of
Lynchburg, TN
Date of Death: Dec 4, 1926 at Bedford County Hospital, Shelbyville, TN
Place of Funeral: County Line, TN
Interred: County Line Cemetery
Date of Birth: May 24, 1882
Age: 44y, 6m, 10d
Color: White – Occupation: Farmer
Married
Birthplace: Moore County, TN
Last place of Residence: County Line, TN
Father: Geo. Hice
Birthplace: Rutherford County, TN

Mother: Sophia Womack
Birthplace: TN
Physician: Dr. J.D. McCord

HIGH, MARY HOLLAND
Date of Funeral: Oct 25, 1927
Casket: Flat Top L.S., size 3/6 & Box $ 28.50
Date of Death: Oct 24, 1927 at 24th District, Bedford County, TN
Place of Funeral: 24th District, Bedford County, TN
Interred: Smiths Chapel
Date of Birth: Jan 20, 1925
Age: 2y, 9m, 4d.
Color: White
Birthplace: Bedford County, TN
Father: W.C. High
Birthplace: Bedford County, TN
Mother: Irene Tinney
Birthplace: Alabama
Physician: Dr. Conditt
Cause of Death: Burns

HILL, JOHN PAXTON, JR.
Date of Funeral: Jun 25, 1927   2:30 p.m.
Casket: White plush, size 2/6 &
Box, Hearse, Services $ 55.00
Metal Box Covers   4.00
Grave Lining   2.00
Total: $ 66.00
Ordered by Mrs. Connie M. Hill, Christianburg, VA
Date of Death: Jun 14, 1927 at Home, Jno. D. Hanson
Place of Funeral: Home of Jno. D. Hanson
Clergyman: Dr. S.P. White & Dr. J.E. Vanse
Interred: Willow Mount Cemetery, Shelbyville, TN
Date of Birth: Nov 20, 1927
Age: 7m, 4d.
Color: White
Birthplace: LaFayette, Louisiana
Last place of Residence: Shelbyville, TN
Father: Jno. P. Hill
Birthplace: Virginia
Mother: Albyne Hanson
Birthplace: Shelbyville, TN
Physician: Dr. Ben L. Burdett

HIMES, ED. P.
Date of Funeral: Oct 14, 1926   11 a.m.
Removing Remains from Wartrace to Shelbyville, TN &
From Shelbyville to New Hope $ 25.00
Metal Box Covers   5.00
Total: $ 30.00
Date of Death: Oct 1, 1926 at Jacksonville, Florida
Place of Funeral: New Hope
Clergyman: Dr. J.W. Cherry
Date of Birth: ____
Age: 55 yrs.
Color: White
Married
No other information.

HIMES, JOHN ALBERT
Date of Funeral: Jan 25, 1929   12:30 p.m.
Embalming: $ 20.00
Casket Oct Gray, plush, size 6/3 &
Box, Hearse, Services   200.00
Burial Garment: Suit, Shirt, Collar, Tie, Hose   30.00
Metal Box Covers   6.00
Total: $256.00
Date of Death: Jan 23, 1929 at Bedford County Hospital, Shelbyville, TN
Place of Funeral: Home, G.F. Himes
Clergyman: Rev. Frank N. Tinder
Interred: New Hope Cemetery
Date of Birth: Dec 7, 1855
Age: 73y, 1m, 16d.
Color: White – Occupation: Practical Nurse
Widower
Birthplace: Bedford County, TN
Father: Grafton Himes
Birthplace: North Carolina
Mother: Nancy Buckingham
Birthplace: Marshall County, TN
Physician: Dr. T.R. Ray

HIMES, MRS. ADDIE RUTH
Date of Funeral: Dec 28, 1926   1 p.m.
Casket: ½ Couch, Gray, Plush, size 6/3 &
Box, Hearse, Services $ 275.00
Burial Garment: Silk Dress   33.50
Metal Box Covers   6.00
Labor to putting up tent   6.00

Total: $ 320.50
Date of Death: Dec 27, 1926 at Home, 23rd District, Bedford County, TN
Place of Home, 23rd District, Bedford County, TN
Clergyman: Bro. S.A. Jones
Date of Birth: Sep 27, 1862
Age: 64y, 3m.
Color: White – Occupation: Housewife
Married
Birthplace: Moore County, TN
Last place of Residence: Bedford County, TN
Husband: Foge Himes
Father: Emyrson Haynes
Birthplace: Moore County, TN
Mother: Margaret Reed
Birthplace: Bedford County, TN
Physician: Dr. T.J. Coble

HITT, MRS. MARY ELLENDER
Date of Funeral: Aug 20, 1926   2 p.m.
Embalming $ 20.00
Casket: Steel Gray B.C., size 6/3 &
Box, ½ Couch, Hearse, Service   275.00
Burial Garment: White Silk Dress   33.00
Slippers, Box Covers, Metal   6.00
Grave Tent, Put-up & Drayage   10.00
Total: $ 343.00
Ordered by Family
Date of Death: Aug 19, 1926 at Home, Shelbyville, TN
Clergyman: Dr. Chas. Armstrong
Interred: Shoffners Chapel, Bedford County, TN
Date of Birth: Jul 29, 1844
Age: 82 yrs.
Color: White – Occupation: Housewife
Widow
Birthplace: Bedford County, TN
Father: Tradell Law
Birthplace: TN
Mother: ____?
Physician: Dr. Ben Burdett

HIX, LAWSON G.
Date of Funeral: May 27 , 1925   2 p.m.
Removing Remains from Train to Church & Cemetery $ 15.00
Metal Box Covers   5.00
Grave Lining   1.50

Drayage, Box, Chairs $ 15.00
Total: $ 22.0
Date of Death: May 24. 1925 at Chicago, Illinois
Place of Funeral: Shelbyville, TN
Clergyman: Dr. Watson
Date of Burial: May 27, 1925
Interred: Willow Mount Cemetery, Shelbyville, TN
Date of Birth: Oct 17, 1882
Age: 42 yrs.
Color: White – Occupation: Salesman
Single
Birthplace: Shelbyville, TN

HIX, SARAH VIVIAN
Date of Funeral: Feb 17, 1927   2:30 p.m.
Casket: Silk P. Couch, size 2/6 & Box
Car, Services $ 85.00
Metal Board   3.00
Total: $ 88.00
Ordered by Claude Hix
Date of Death: Feb 17, 1927 at 23rd District, Bedford County, TN
Interred: Flat Creek Cemetery
Date of Birth: Oct 11, 1925
Age: 1y, 4 m.
Birthplace: 23rd District, Bedford County, TN
Father: Claude Hix
Birthplace: Bedford County, TN
Mother: Louise Love
Birthplace: Rutherford County, TN
Physician: Dr. Conditt

HIX, W.W.
Date of Funeral: Oct 27, 1926   2 p.m.
Embalming, Converty $ 10.00
Casket: Sil Gray B C, size 6/3   300.00
Outside Case: Cedar   25.00
Suit, Underwear, Sox   2.50
Total: $ 343.50
Date of Death: Oct 26, 1926 at 23rd District, Bedford County, TN
Place of Funeral: Flat Creek, TN
Clergyman: Dr. Geo. Gowan
Interred: Hix Grave Yard
Date of Birth: Jan 20, 1858
Age: 68 yrs.
Color: White – Occupation: Farmer

Married
Birthplace: Bedford County, TN
Father: Wm. S. Hix
Birthplace: TN
Mother: Martha Ann Word
Birthplace: Bedford County, TN
Physician: Dr. Conditt

HOLDER, FRANCIS ILOE

Date of Funeral: Dec 5, 1924 2 p.m.	
Embalming	$ 15.00
Casket: White, plush, size 4/6	90.00
Drayage, Metal Box Covers	4.00
Grave Lining	1.50
Total	$110.50

Date of Death: Dec 4, 1924 at Shelbyville, TN
Place of Funeral: Home, Shelbyville, TN
Clergyman: Bro _____(?)
Interred: Willow Mount Cemetery, Shelbyville, TN
Date of Birth: Mar 29, 1918
Age: 6y, 8m, 5d.
Color"White
Birthplace: Roanoak. Alabama
Last place of Residence: Shelbyville, TN
Father: Wm. R. Holder
Birthplace: Randolph County, Alabama
Mother: Myrtle Avery Holder
Birthplace: Randolph County, Alabama
Physician: Dr. Avery

HOLLIBURTON, CHAS.

Date of Funeral: Jan 26, 1928 2 p.m.	
Casket: County, size 6/3	$ 12.50

Date of Death: Jan 26, 1928 at Home, Shelbyville, TN
Place of Funeral: Home, Shelbyville, TN
Clergyman: Rev. E.P. Watson
Interred: Willow Mount Cemetery, Shelbyville, TN
Date of Birth: Dec 6, 1896
Age: 34y, 1m, 18d.
Color: White – Occupation: Laborer
Father: Chas. Holliburton
Birthplace: Unknown
Mother: Unknown
Birthplace: Unknown
Physician: Dr. Jas. L. Morton

HOLT, JOHN EARL
Date of Funeral: May 21, 1926   11:30 a.m.
Removing Remains from Train to Cemetery $ 15.00
Metal Grave Corners   5.00
Grave Lining   2.00
Total: $ 22.00
Ordered by Dr. T.J. Coble
Date of Death: Birmingham, Alabama
Place of Funeral: Willow Mount Cemetery, Shelbyville, TN
Clergyman: Dr. J.W. Cherry
Date of Birth: ____
Age: 40 yrs.
Color: White – Occupation: Salesman
Birthplace: Shelbyville, TN

HOLT, WILLIAM EARLE
Date of Funeral: Jun 10, 1929   1 p.m.
Casket: Flat Top L.S., size 3/6 $ 45.00
Box, Metals, Hearse, Service, Ambulance   56.00
Total $100.00
Date of Death: Jun 9, 1020 at Bedford County Hospital
Place of Funeral: Home
Clergyman: Cunningham
Interred: Cotton Mill, Bedford County, TN
Date of Birth: Mar 14 1926
Age: 3y, 2m, 26d.
Color: White
Birthplace: Bedford County, TN
Father: Hardie Holt
Birthplace: Rutherford County, TN
Mother: Leona Gray
Birthplace: Alabama
Physician: Dr. Jas. L. Morton

HORNADAY (Infant of Mr. and Mrs. Joe Hornaday)
Date of Funeral: Jul 15, 1926
Casket: Flat op L.S., size 2.0 & Box, Hearse $ 15.00
Date of Death: Hospital, Shelbyville, TN
Place of Funeral: Shofner Grave Yard
Interred: Shoffner Grave Yard
Date of Birth: Jul 14, 1926
Age: 0
Color: White
Birthplace: Hospital, Shelbyville, TN
Father: Joe Hornaday

Mother: ____
Physician: Dr. T.J. Coble
Cause of Death: Stillborn

HOUSTON, MRS. BLANCHE VENERABLE
Date of Funeral: Mar 11, 1926   10:30 a.m.
Casket: Gray E. Crane, size 5/9 &
Box, Hearse, Services $ 125.00
Burial Garment: Gray Silk Dress   20.00
Meal Box Covers   5.00
Total $ 150.00
Ordered by Miss Corenne Houston
Date of Death: Mar 9, 1926 at Home, Shelbyville, TN
Place of Funeral: Home, Shelbyville, TN
Clergyman: Dr. J.W. Cherry
Interred: Houston Grave Yard
Date of Birth: Don't know.
Age: About 79 yrs.
Widow
Birthplace: Winchester, TN
Last place of Residence: Shelbyville, TN
Husband: Robert L. Houston
Father: W.E. Venerable
Birthplace: Virginia
Mother: Jane Curl
Birthplace: Winchester, TN

HOUSTON, ROBERT WORK
Date of Funeral: Dec 2, 1925   2 p.m.
Casket: Blk E. Crape. Size 6/3 &
Box, Hearse, Services $ 100.00
Blk B.C. Suit   30.00
Metal Box Covers   5.00
Total: $135 .00
Date of Death: Dec 1, 1925 at Home, Shelbyville, TN
Place of Funeral: Home, Shelbyville, TN
Clergyman: Dr. J.W. Cherry & Dr. S.P. White
Interred: Houston Grave Yard
Date of Birth: Dec 28, 1838
Age: 86 yrs.
Married
Birthplace: Bedford County, TN
Father: Caleb F. Houston
Mother: Jane Work
Physician: Dr. T.J. Coble

HOWARD, MRS. ROSIE
Date of Funeral: Mar 3, 1925   2 p.m.
Casket: Whitte, P.K., size 6/0 & Box, Services $ 100.00
Ordered by Henry Howard
No other information

HOWARD, PAULINE
Date of Funeral: Jul 20, 1928   4 p.m.
Casket: White L.S., flat Top, size 3/6 & Box $ 35.00
Date of Death: Jul 20, 1928 at Home, 22nd District, Bedford County, TN
Place of Funeral: Mt. Herman
Clergyman: Elder Jesse Hart
Interred: Mt. Herman Cemetery
Date of Birth: Oct 23, 1926
Age: 1y, 8m, 27d.
Color: White
Birthplace: Bedford County, TGN
Father: Ollie Howard
Birthplace: ____
Mother: Clara Weaver
Birthplace: ____
Physician: Dr. Jno. Sutton

HOYT, MRS. SALLIE
Date of Funeral: Jan 12, 1925   2 p.m.
Removing Remains from Central State Hospital,
at Nashville, TN to Shelbyville $ 25.00
Casket: Blk., Eng. Gray, size 6/3   110.00
Burial Garment: Blk. Dress   15.00
Drayage   1.00
Grave Lining   1.50
Total: $ 152.50
Ordered by F.J. Wallheiser
Date of Death: Jan 11, 1925 at 5:30 a.m.
Place of Death: Central State Hospital, Nashville, TN
Place of Funeral: Shelbyville, TN
Clergyman: Dr. Robinson
Interred: Willow Mount Cemetery, Shelbyville, TN
Date of Birth: ____
Age: 75 yrs.
Color: White
Father: Edmond Cooper
No other information

HUDSON, MARY FRANCIS
Date of Funeral: Feb 18, 1926   11 a.m.
Casket: Chatt. White, , size 4/6 &
Hearse, Box, Services $ 60.00
Burial Garment: Underwear, Hose, Blanket   3.00
Total: $ 63.00
Ordered by Wiley Hudson
Date of Death: Feb 17, 1926 at Bedford County Hospital, Shelbyville, TN
Place of Funeral: Holland Grave yard
Clergyman: Dr. J.P. Robertson
Interred: Holland Grave Yard
Date of Birth: Mar 16, 1921
Age: 5yrs.
Color: White
Birthplace: Bedford County, TN
Father: Wiley Hudson
Mother: ____
Physician: Dr. W.H. Avery
Cause of Death: Burned

HUTSON, JAMES L.
Date of Funeral: Sep 21, 1927   10 a.m.
Embalming: $ 20.00
Casket: 1010 Gray B.C., size 6/3 &
Hearse, Services   325.00
Metal Vault, Style, Clark   125.00
Total: $470.00
Ordered by Mrs. Gammill & R.S. Hutson
Date of Death: Sep 20, 1927 at Home, near Flat Creek, TN
Place of Funeral: Near Flat Creek, TN
Clergyman: rev. Geo. Gowan
Interred: Flat reek Cemetery
Date of Birth: Mar 15, 1852
Age: 75y, 6m, 4d.
Color: White – Occupation: Civil Engineer
Married
Birthplace: Bedford County, TN
Father: Tom Hutson
Birthplace: Bedford County, TN
Mother: Mary Hazlett
Birthplace: Bedford County, TN
Physician: Dr. Conditt

INGLE, MRS. VIRGINIA ALICE

Date of Funeral: May 22, 2927   4 p.m.

Embalming	$ 20.00
Casket: State, ½ Couch, size 6/3 &	
Gray B.C., Batesville	440.00
Burial Garment: Silk Dress	30.00
Slippers	4.00
Clark Vault	125.00
Grave Lining	3.50
Total:	$ 622.50

Ordered by Family

Date of Death: May 21, 1927 at Home, Shelbyville, TN

Place of Funeral: Baptist Church, Shelbyville, TN

Clergy: Dr. S.P. White

Interred: Willow Mount Cemetery, Shelbyville. TN

Date of Birth: Aug 6, 1854

Age: 72y, 9m, 14d.

Color: White – Occupation: Housewife

Widow

Birthplace: Coffee County, TN

Last place of Residence: Shelbyville, TN

Husband: Samuel Heard

Birthplace of Birth: ____

Mother: Mary Hiles

Birthplace: Bedford County, TN

Physician: Dr. W.H. Avery

IVIE; THOMPSON B.

Date of Funeral: Sep 6, 1928   11:15 a.m.

Casket: Oct Gray Plush, size 6/3 &	
Box, Hearse, Service	$ 200.00
Grave Lining	3.00
Cemetery Bill	7.50
Metal Box Covers	6.00
Henry H. Grueter, Bill	80.82
Total:	$ 296.82
Sale:	$ 209.00

Ordered by Chas. S. Ivie

Date pf Death: Sep 4, 1928 at General Hospital, Cincinnati, Ohio

Place of Funeral: Willow Mount Cemetery, Shelbyville, TN

Clergyman: Dr. J.S. Sibley

Interred: Willow Mount Cemetery, Shelbyville, TN

Date of Birth: 48y, 1m, 23d.

Color: White – Occupation: Printer

Widower, Divorced

Birthplace: Bedford County, TN
Last place of Residence: Cincinnati, Ohio
Father: Wells W. Ivie
Birthplace: Bedford County, TN
Other: Betty Miller Ivie
Birthplace: Bedford County, TN

JENKINS (Infant of T.C. Jenkins(COL)
Date of Funeral: Jul 1, 1925
Casket: White P.K., size 2/6 & Box $ 25.00
Ordered by Sam Jenkins (Jno. Hall)
Date of Death: Jul 1, 1925 at 9ᵗʰ District, Bedford County, TN
Interred: Blankenship Cemetery
Date of Birth: ____
Age: 6m.
Color: Colored
Father: T.C. Jenkins
Mother: ____
Physician: Dr. A.N. Gordon

JENKINS, MRS. ANNIE MOORE
Date of Funeral: Dec 3, 1928   2 p.m.
Embalming: $ 20.00
Casket: Batesville Gray Steel, size 6/3 &
Hearse, Personal Service   645.00
Outside Case, Cedar   35.00
Metal Box Covers   6.00
Total: $ 706.00
Date of Death: Dec 2, 1928 at Home of Clarence Snell, Shelbyville, TN
Clergyman: Rev. J.W. Cherry, J.S. Sibley & Chas. Armstrong
Date of Death: Dec 3, 1928
Interred: Jenkins Chapel Cemetery
Date of Birth: Feb 14, 1886
Age: 46y, 9m, 18d.
Color: White – Occupation: Housewife
Widow
Birthplace: Bedford County, TN
Father: Arch G. Moore
Birthplace: Bedford County, TN
Mother: Mattie Tune
Birthplace: Bedford County, TN
Physician: Dr. T.R. Ray

JOHNSON, HORACE CLAUDE
Date of Funeral: May 10, 1929   2 p.m.
Casket: Oct E Crape, Chott., size 6/3
Box, Hearse, Services $ 100.00
Burial Garment: Suit, Shirt, Collar, Tie   19.00
Metal Box Covers   6.00
Grave Lining   3.00
Underwear, Sox   2.00
Total: $ 130.00

Date of Death: May 9, 1929at Home, Wartrace Pike, Shelbyville, TN
Place of Funeral: Home, Wartrace Pike, Shelbyville, TN
Clergyman: Rev. Frank Finder
Interred: Willow Mount Cemetery, Shelbyville, TN
Date of Birth: Jan 23, 1899
Age: 30y, 4m, 15d.
Color: White – Occupation: Carpenter
Married
Birthplace: Rutherford County, TN
Last place of Residence: Shelbyville, TN
Father: W.M. Johnson
Birthplace: Rutherford County, TN
Mother: Emma Arnold
Birthplace: Cannon County, TN
Physician: Dr. Ben L. Bartlett

JOHNSON, JAMES GILBERT
Date of Funeral: Jul 4, 1929   10:30 a.m.
Casket: Oct L.S., size 3/2 &
Box, Metals, Hearse, Services $ 45.00
Date of Death: Jul 3, 1929 at Home, Wartrace Pike, Shelbyville
Place of Funeral: Home, Wartrace Pile, Shelbyville, TN
Clergyman: Rev. Creasman
Interred: Willow Mount Cemetery, Shelbyville, TN
Date of Birth: Apr 21, 1927
Age: 2y, 2m, 11d.
Color: White
Birthplace: Bedford County, TN
Father: Claude Johnson (Deceased)
Birthplace: Rutherford County, TN
Mother: Winnie Reed
Birthplace: Bedford County, TN
Physician: Dr. W.H. Avery

JOHNSON, SAM HOUSTON
Date of Funeral: Jam 29. 1926   2 p.m.
Removing Remains from B. Johnson's home $ 10.00
Embalming: 20.00
Casket: State Gray B.C., size 6/3, hinge cap &
Hearse, Box, Services   325.00
Metal Vault, Style: Clark   125.00
Total: $480.00
Date of Death: Jan 17, 1926 at Bedford County, TN
Place of Funeral: Home, Bedford County, N
Date of Burial: Jan 19, 1926

Interred at Lutheran Church
Date of Birth: Jan 15, 1849
Age: 77 yrs.
Color: White – Occupation: Farmer
Birthplace: Jefferson, Texas
Last place of Residence: Bedford County, TN
Father: Wm. Johnson
Birthplace: ____
Mother: ____
Birthplace: Texas
Physician: Dr. T.J. Coble

JOHNSTON, FOUNTAIN BASCOM
Date of Funeral: Jan 22, 1928   1:30 p.m.
Casket: B., size 5/9
Box, Hearse, Services, Robe $ 50.00
Date of Death: Jan 21, 1928 at 6th District, Bedford County, TN
Interred: Burns Cemetery
Clergyman: Not Any
Date of Birth: Jul 4, 1844
Age: 83y, 6m, 17d.
Color: White
Widower
Birthplace: Jackson County, TN
Last place of Residence: Bedford County, TN
Father: Milas (?) Johnston
Birthplace: Jackson County, TN
Mother: Susan Ray
Birthplace: Jackson County, TN
Physician: Dr. Jas. L. Morton

JONES, DR. SAMUEL ROBERT
Date of Funeral: Aug 28, 1827   3 p.m.
Casket: Gray B.C., State, size 6/3 &
Hearse, Box, Services $ 325.00
Metal Box Covers   6.00
Grave Lining   3.50
Total: $ 334.50
                          (illegible) 9/2   20.00
Total: $ 354.50
Ordered by Mrs. Myrtle Jones
Date of Death: Aug 27, 1927 at Tullahoma, TN
Place of Funeral: Home, Shelbyville TN
Clergyman: Mr. J.A. Tate & Bro. J.W. Cherry
Interred: Willow Mount Cemetery, Shelbyville, TN

Date of Birth: Sep 18, 1847
Age: 49y, 11m, 9d.
Color: White – Occupation: Dentist
Married
Birthplace: Bedford County, TN
Father: T.J. Jones
Birthplace: Lincoln County, TN
Mother: Mary Harrison
Birthplace: Bedford County, TN
Physician: Dr. Mitchell, Tullahoma, TN

JONES, FRANCIS PAUL
Date Funeral: Sep 26, 1926   2 p.m.
Casket: Blk E. rape, size 6/3 &
Suit, Hearse, Services $ 100.00
Outside Case, Cedar   25.00
Total: $ 125.00
Ordered by Sons
Date of Death: Sep 25, 1926 at Home, 9th District, Bedford County, TN
Interred: Jones – Haynes Grave Yard
Date of Birth: Jan 22, 184
Age: 82 yrs.
Color: White – Occupation: Farmer
Birthplace: Bedford County, TN
Father: Simeon W. Jones
Birthplace: ____
Mother: Lucindia Primrose
Birthplace: ____
Physician: Dr. A.N. Gordon

JONES, JAMES WILLIAM
Date of Funeral: Apr 29, 1926   10 a.m.
Casket: White L.S., Flat Top, size 2/0 &
Box, Services $ 15.00
Date of Death: Apr 28, 1926 at Home, Shelbyville, TN
Place of Funeral: Naz. Church, Shelbyville, TN
Clergyman: Dr. Robertson
Date of Birth: Apr 28, 1926
Age: 0
Color: White
Birthplace: Home, Shelbyville, TN
Father: Rev. S.A. Jones
Birthplace: TN
Mother: Bertha Nanie (?) Jones
Birthplace: TN

Physician: Dr. W.H. Avery

JONES, MRS. BERTHA SHODOAN(?) NANCE
Date of Funeral: May 6, 1926   10 a.m.
Embalming $ 20.00
Casket: Nat. White plush, size 6/3x &
Box, Hearse, Services   200.00
Burial Garment: Crepe D. Dress, Hose, Slippers   25.00
Metal Box Covers   5.00
Total: $ 250.00
Ordered by Rev. S.A. Jones
Date of Death: May 4, 1926 at Bedford County Hospital, Shelbyville, TN
Place of Funeral: Church, Shelbyville, TN
Clergyman: Bro. Wyse
Interred: Willow Mount Cemetery, Shelbyville, TN
Date of Birth: Jul 25, 1898
Age: 27yrs.
Color: White – Occupation: Housewife
Married
Birthplace: Murray County, TN (Maury Co.)
Last place of Residence: Shelbyville, TN
Husband: S.A. Jones
Father: J.H. Nance
Birthplace: TN
Mother: Georgia Johnson
Birthplace: TN
Physician: Dr. W.H. Avery

JONES, MRS. MARY STACY
Date of Funeral: Jan 12, 1928   2 p.m.
Casket: Oct White, L.S., size 6/3 &
Box, Hearse, Grave Lining, Metals, Service $ 125.00
Date of Death: Jan 11, 1928 at Home, Shelbyville, TN
Place of Funeral: Shelbyville, TN
Clergyman: Bro. J.W. Cherry
Interred: Willow Mount Cemetery, Shelbyville, TN
Date of Birth: May 17, 1890
Age: 37y, 7m, 15d.
Color: White – Occupation: Housewife
Married
Birthplace: Bedford County, TN
Husband: Chas. Jones
Father: Jno. Deason
Birthplace: Bedford County, TN
Mother: Alice Brown

Birthplace: Bedford County, TN
Physician: Dr. Jas. L. Morton

JONES, WILLIAM HARDEN
Date of Funeral: Apr 24, 1925   2:30 p.m.
Casket: Gray, B.., State, size 6/3 $ 325.00
Cedar Box   25.00
Metal Box Covers   5.00
Drayage & etc.   3.50
Total: $ 358.50
Ordered by Mrs. Kate Jones
Date of Death: Apr 22, 1925 at Shelbyville, TN
Place of Funeral: Home, Shelbyville, TN
Clergyman: Dr. J.W. Cherry
Interred: Willow Mount Cemetery, Shelbyville, TN
Date of Birth: Dec 7, 1867
Age: ____
Color: White – Occupation: Salesman
Married
Physician: Dr. T.J. Coble

JORDAN, WILLIAM COLEMAN
Date of Funeral: Dec 12, 1927   10 a.m.
Embalming $ 20.00
Casket: Oct Gray, E. Crape, size 6/3 &
Hearse, Box, Services   125.00
Burial Garment: Suit   31.00
Underwear, Sox   2.00
Metal Box Covers   6.00
Total: $ 184.00
Date of Death: Dec 10, 1927 at Home, Shelbyville, TN
Place of Funeral: Methodist Church, Shelbyville, TN
Clergyman: Bro. J.W. Cherry
Interred: Burns Cemetery
Date of Birth: Mar 16, 1868
Age: 59y, 8m, 24d.
Color: White – Occupation: Clerk
Married
Birthplace: Bedford County, TN
Father: Wm. A. Jordan
Birthplace: Williamson County, TN
Mother: Susan Chunn
Birthplace: Bedford County, TN
Physician: Dr. Jas. L. Morton

KELLY, MRS. SARAH ZANZALINE
Date of Funeral: Mar 24, 1924   10 a.m.
Casket: White, Plush, size 6/0 & Box, Hearse, Services $ 175,00
Burial Garment: White Crape Dress   25.00
Slippers   3.00
Hose   2.00
Metal Box Covers   5.00
Total: $ 210.00
Date of Death: Mar 2, 1926(24?) at Whitthorne Street, Shelbyville, TN
Place of Funeral: Whitthorne Street, Shelbyville, TN
Clergyman: Dr. E.P. Watson
Interred: Willow Mount Cemetery, Shelbyville, TN
Date of Birth: Jan 24, 1858
Age: 68 yrs.
Color: White – Occupation: House wife
Widow
Birthplace: Hickman County, TH
Father: Wm. Thornton
Birthplace: ____
Mother: ____
Physician: Dr. Fuston

KENT, ISAAC GARFIELD
Date of Funeral: Apr 20. 1925   11 a.m.
Removing Remains from Shelbyville to Fosterville $ 10.00
Embalming   15.00
Casket: Sil Plush, size 6/3 & Box, Services   185.00
Total: $225.00
Ordered by W.E. Smith & Jim Parker
Date of Death: Apr 19, 1925 at Shelbyville, TN
Place of Funeral: Fosterville, TN
Clergyman: Dr. White & Dr. Watson
Interred: Near Fosterville, TN
Date of Birth: Jun 14, 1896
Age: 29 yrs.
Color: White – Occupation: Public Works
Married
Birthplace: TN
Physician: Dr. Jas. Morton

KEY, MRS. ETHEL
Date of Funeral: Dec 28, 1927   2 p.m.
Casket: Oct Gray, E. Crape, size 5/9 &
Box, Hearse, Services $ 125.00
Burial Garment: Silk Winding Sheet   20.00

Slippers	$ 5.00
Metal Box Covers	6.00
Grave Lining	3.00
Total:	$159.00

Date of Death: Dec 27, 1927 at Home, Shelbyville, TN
Place of Funeral: Home, Shelbyville, TN
Date of Burial: Dec 28, 1927
Interred: Willow Mount Cemetery, Shelbyville, TN
Date of Birth: Sep 9, 1885
Age: 42y, 3m, 17 d.
Color: White – Occupation: Housewife
Married
Birthplace: Bedford County, TN
Father: Jno. Melson
Birthplace: Bedford County, TN
Mother: Julia Patterson
Birthplace: Bedford County, TN
Physician: Dr. Jas. Morton

KIMBRO, DEWEY DEAN
Date of Funeral: Sep 25, 1926   2 p.m.
Casket: White, plush State coach, size 4/6 &

Hearse, Services	$ 150.00
Metal Vault, Style, Clark	100.00
Total:	$ 250.00

Ordered by Jim Kimbro
Date of Death: Sep 24, 1926 at Home of Jim Kimbro
Place of Funeral: Home of Jim Kimbro
Clergyman: Dr. J.E. Vanse & Dr. S.P. White
Interred: Willow Mount Cemetery, Shelbyville, TN
Date of Birth: Aug 4, 1921
Age: 5yrs.
Color: White
Birthplace: Flat Creek, TN
Last place of Resident: Mississippi
Father: Dewey H. Kimbro
Birthplace: Bedford County, County, TN
Mother: Addie Delk
Birthplace: Bedford County, TN
Physician: Dr. Conditt

KIMBRO, JAMES ALEXANDER
Date of Funeral: Feb 28, 1927   3 p.m.
Embalming $ 20.00
Casket: State Gray B.C., size 6/3 &

Hearse, Service	$325.00
Metal Vault, Style, Clark	125.00
Burial Garment: Suit, Collar, Tie	32.00
Hose	.75
Grave Lining	2.00
Total:	$ 504.75

Date of Death: Feb 26, 1927 at Home, 23rd District, Bedford County, TN
Place of Funeral: Singleton Christian Church
Interred: Willow Mount Cemetery, Shelbyville, TN
Date of Birth: Sep 6, 1858
Age: 68y, 5m, 20d.
Color: White – Occupation: Farmer
Married
Birthplace: Bedford County, TN
Father: Riley Kimbro
Birthplace: Bedford County, TN
Physician: Dr. T.R. Ray

KIMMONS, JOHN DAVIDSON
Date of Funeral: Jan 10, 1929   2:30 p.m.
Casket: Oct Gray, Plush, size: 6/3 &

Hearse, Services	$ 250.00
Metal Vault, Style, Clark	125.00
Grave Lining	6.00
Drayage, Chairs, Tent, etc.	3.50
Ambulance	15.00
Flowers	13.50
Cemetery	7.50
Total:	$ 420.50

Ordered by Dr. A.J. Kimmons
Date of Death: Jan 9, 1929 at Home, 20th District, Bedford County, TN
Place of Funeral: Willow Mount Cemetery, Shelbyville, TN
Clergyman: Rev. Geo. Gowan
Interred: Willow Mount Cemetery, Shelbyville, TN
Date of Birth: Dec 1, 1852
Age: 76y, 1m, 9d.
Color: White – Occupation: Farmer
Widower
Birthplace: Bedford County, TN
Father: Joshua Kimmons
Birthplace: Bedford County, TN
Mother: Isabell McClintock
Birthplace: Bedford County, TN
Physician: Dr. Ben L. Burdett

KIMMONS, MRS. ANN
Date of Funeral: Jan 15, 1925
Casket: Sil Gray, Crape, size 6/3 $ 125.00
Burial Garment: Ladies White Robe   5.00
Total: $ 130.00
Ordered by C.E. Crowell & H.D. Crowell &
Mrs. Fannie Crowell
Place of Funeral: Bedford County, TN
Interred: _____
Date of Birth: ____
Age: 75 yrs.
Color: White
Widow
Birthplace: Coffee County, TN
Physician: Dr. Fuston

KIMMONS, MRS. MARY WELLINGTON
Date of Funeral: Feb 9, 1927   10 a.m.
Removing Remains from Train $ 15.00
Grave Lining   2.00
Metal Boards   6.00
Truck Driver   2.00
Total: $ 25.00
Date of Death: Feb 7, 1927 at Nashville TN
Place of Funeral: Shelbyville, TN
Clergyman: Dr. S.P. White
Interred: Willow Mount Cemetery, Shelbyville, TN
Date of Birth: ____
Age: 65 yrs.
Color: White – Occupation: Housewife
Widow
Birthplace: ____
Last place of Residence: Nashville, TN

KIMREY, JAMES ALLEN
Date of Funeral: Feb 20, 1927   2:30 p.m.
Casket: White Plush, size 2/0 &
Box, Chairs, Service $ 50.00
Date of Death: Feb 19, 1927 at Home, Shelbyville, TN
Place of Funeral: Home, Shelbyville, TN
Clergyman: J.W. Cherry
Interred: Willow Mount Cemetery, Shelbyville, TN
Date of Birth: Dec 19, 1927
Age: 2m,
Color: White

Birthplace: Shelbyville, TN
Father: W.F. Kimery
Birthplace: Bedford County, TN
Mother: Burdie Philpot
Birthplace: Bedford County, TN
Physician: Dr. W.H. Avery

KIRKPATRICK, MRS. MATTIE
Date of Funeral: Jan 10, 1929   3:30 p.m.
Removing Remains from Train, Depot $ 13.00
Date of Death: Jan 9, 1929 at Alabama City, Alabama
Place of Funeral: Alabama City, Alabama
Clergyman: Rev. Frank Tinder, Shelbyville, TN
Interred: Willow Mount, Cemetery, Shelbyville, TN
Date of Birth: ____
Age: 51 yrs.
Color: White – Occupation: Housewife
No other information.

LACY, CALLLIE FLORENCE
Date of Funeral: Jun 30, 1929   4:30 p.m.
Embalming $ 20.00
Casket: Oct Gray, E. Crape, size: 6/3x &
Box, Hearse, Services   150.00
Metal Box Covers   6.00
(illegible)   4.00
Total: $ 180.00
Ordered by Thomas H. Lacy
Date of Death: Jun 29, 1929 at Home, Shelbyville, TN
Place of Funeral: Home, Shelbyville, TN
Clergyman: Rev. J.S. Sibley
Interred: Willow Mount Cemetery, Shelbyville, TN
Date of Birth: Mar 1, 1877
Age: 52y, 2m, 29d.
Color: White – Occupation: Housewife
Married
Birthplace: Bedford County, TN
Husband: T.H. Lacy
Father: H.M. Head
Birthplace: Bedford County, N
Mother: Buna Vista Gambill
Birthplace: Mississippi
Physician: Dr. Jas. L. Morton

LACY, WALLACE W.
Date of Funeral: Jun 2, 1925   3 p.m.
Embalming $ 15.00
Casket: Blk. B.C., State, size 6/3   285.00
Box, Services & Metal Box Covers   5.00
Total: $ 305.00
Ordered by Family
Date of Death: Jun 1, 1925 at Shelbyville, TN
Place of Funeral: Shelbyville, TN
Clergyman: Dr. Robinson
Interred: Willow Mount Cemetery, Shelbyville, TN
Date of Birth May 15, 1847
Age: 78 yrs.
Color: White
Birthplace: TN
Physician: Dr. Burdett

LANDERS, MRS. ANN
Date of Funeral: Dec 13, 1925   1 p.m.
Casket: B.C. Coffin, size 6/0 &

Box, Hearse, Personal Services: $ 65.00
Date of Death: Dec 12, 1925 at County Line, Bedford County, TN
Interred: Burns Cemetery, Bedford County, TN
Date of Birth: Dec 25, 1839
Age: 86 yrs.
Color: White – Occupation: Not Any
Birthplace: Bedford County, TN
Father: Jessie Clanton
Physician: Dr. T.R. Ray

LANE, MISS DAISIE
Date of Funeral: Nov 17, 1929   2:30 p.m.
Removal Remains: 1 Trip from Depot to J.D. Hutton (Hutson?) and to the
Cemetery: $ 20.00
Grave Lining   6.00
Metal Box Covers   6.00
Drayage, etc   3.00
Total: $ 35.00
Date of Death: Nov 15, 1928 at Edgehill Sanitorium, Knoxville, TN
Place of Funeral: J.D. Hutton(?), Sr., Shelbyville, TN
Clergyman: Dr. J.S. Sibley
Interred: Willow Mount Cemetery, Shelbyville, TN
Date of Birth: ____
Age: 52 yrs.
Color: White
Single
Father: Wm. Lane

LANGLEY, MRS. SALLLIE E.
Date of Funeral: Mar 1, 1927   2 p.m.
Embalming: $ 20.00
Casket: Gray Oak, E. crape, size 5/9   125.00
Metal Box Covers   6.00
Total: $151.00
Date of Death: Feb 28, 1927 at Home, F.R. Bearden, Shelbyville, TN
Place of Funeral: Cemetery at Murfreesboro, TN
Clergyman: Dr. S.P. White
Interred: Murfreesboro, TN
Date of Birth: Jan 21, 1848
Age: 79 y, 1m, 7d.
Color: White – Occupation: Housewife
Married
Birthplace: Rutherford County, TN
Father: Payton McAdoo
Birthplace: Rutherford County, TN

Mother: Christine Spain
Birthplace: Rutherford County, TN
Physician: Dr. T.R. Ray

LEE, (Infant of Mr. & Mrs. R.H. Lee
Date of Funeral: Jan 5, 1925   11 a.m.
Casket: White, P.K., size 2/0 $ 23.00
Date of Death: Jan 4, 1925 at Shelbyville, TN
Interred: Willow Mount Cemetery, Shelbyville, TN
Birthplace: Shelbyville, TN
No other information

LENTZ, PARKER
Date of Funeral: Apr 6, 1926   11:30 a.m.
Casket: Gray Crape, size 6/3 &
Box, Hearse, Services, $ 120.00
Date of death: Apr 5, 1926 at 18th District, Bedford County, TN
Place of Funeral: Mt. Lebanon, TN
Interred: Mt. Lebanon Cemetery
Date of Birth: Jan 28, 1911
Age: 15 yrs.
Color: White – Occupation: School Boy
Single
Birthplace: Bedford County, TN
Father: R.L. Lentz
Willie Ellie Neely
Physician: Dr. J.L. Morton

LOKEY, J.W.
Date of Funeral: Feb 11, 1925   2 p.m.
Casket: Blk. Eng Crape, size 6/3 &
Metal Covers, Box, Embalming $ 100.00
Date of Death: Feb 10, 1925 at Shelbyville, TN
Place of Funeral: Shelbyville, TN
Clergyman: Dr. S.P. White
Interred: Holland Yard
Date of Birth: ____
Age: 71 yrs.
Color: White – Occupation: Engineer (Station)
Widower
Birthplace: Bedford County, TN
Physician: Dr. Morton

LOWE, MRS. MATTIE
Date of Funeral: Feb 17, 1929   2 p.m.

Casket: E. Sil. Gray, plush, size 5/9 &
Service, Box, Hearse, Dress, Hose, Slippers, Services $250.00
Ordered by L.O. Lowe
Date of Death: Feb 16, 1929 at Home of Son, Bedford County, TN
Place of Burial: Bedford
Clergyman: Rev. Agee
Interred: Bedford Cemetery
Date of Birth: Aug 25 1853
Age: 75y, 5m, 2d.
Color: White – Occupation: Housewife
Widow
Birthplace: Bedford County, TN
Husband: Leoper B. Lowe
Father: W.J. Loyd
Birthplace: TN
Mother: Rhoda Ann Shelton
Birthplace: Bedford County, TN
Physician: Dr. W.H. Avery

LOYD, MRS. EULA BRYANT WAGSTER
Date of Funeral: Nov 27, 1929 at Tullahoma 10 a.m. &
Shelbyville at 12 Noon
Removing Remains from Train to Bill Bryant home
From Tullahoma to Shelbyville $ 25.00
Grave Lining   3.00
Metal Box Covers   6.00
Drayage, Tent, Chairs etc   3.50
Cemetery: $7.50
Total: 37.50
Date of Death: Nov 25, 1929 at Toledo, Ohio
Place of Funeral: Tullahoma & Shelbyville, TN
Clergyman: Rev. Jackson, Tullahoma & Rev. W.C. Cressemon(?),
Shelbyville, TN
Interred: Willow Mount Cemetery, Shelbyville, TN
Age: 21y, 10m, 3d.
Married
Husband: Randolph L. Loyd

LOYD, THELMA CHRISTINE
Date of Funeral: Sep 21, 1925   11 a.m.
Casket: White P.K., size 6/3 &
Box, Hearse, Services $ 100.00
Crepe D.C. , Dress   20.00
Total: $ 120.00
Date of Death: Sep 20, 1925 at Shelbyville, TN

Place of Funeral: Harts Chapel, TN
Clergyman: Bro. Kerney
Interred: Harts Chapel Cemetery
Date of Birth: Jun 16, 1908
Age: 17 yrs.
Color: White – Occupation: Works at Pencil Mill
Married
Birthplace: TN
Father: Geo. Overcast
Physician: Dr. Avery
No other information

LINDSEY, JAMES
Date of Funeral: Feb 1, 1926
Casket: Blk, E. rape, size 5.9 &

Box, Hearse, Services	$ 100.00
Burial Garment: Robe	6.50
Metal Box Covers	5.00
Suit, Underwear, Sox	2.00
Total:	$ 113.50

Date of Death: Jan 30, 1926 at Home, Shelbyville, TN
Place of Funeral: Home, Shelbyville, TN
Clergyman: Dr. Cherry
Interred: Willow Mount Cemetery, Shelbyville, TN
Date of Birth: Sep 29, 1842
Age: 83 yrs.
Color: White – Occupation: Farmer
Married
Birthplace: Georgia
Physician: Dr. Ben Burdett

LUNA, MRS. LUCY
Date of Funeral: Apr 3, 1929   11 a.m.
Casket: Oct Blk., E. Crape, size 5/4 &
Box, Metals, Lining, Services, Hearse $ 125.00
Date of Death: Apr 2, 1929   2 a.m.
Place of Funeral: Loan Oak Cemetery, Lewisburg, TN
Clergyman: Bro. Isom
Interred: Lone Oak Cemetery, Lewisburg, TN
Date of Birth: Jul 29, 1850
Age: 78y, 8m, 4d.
Color: White – Occupation: Housewife
Widow
Birthplace: Marshall County, TN
Last place of Residence: Shelbyville, TN

Husband: John C. Luna
Father: Dillard Petty
Birthplace: Marshall County, TN
Mother: Unknown
Physician: Dr. W.H. Avery

LYNCH, MRS. MARY EVA
Date of Funeral: Dec 25, 1929   2 p.m.
Removing Remains, Embalming,
Casket: Oct Gray plush, size 6/3, Cedar Box,
Hearse, Ambulance, Lining, Dress, Metals,
Hose, Underwear, Services & Truck: $ 275.00
Date of Death: Dec 23, 1929 at Bedford County Hospital
Place of Funeral: Christian Church, Bell Buckle, TN
Clergyman: Rev. Clyde Gleaves
Interred: Bell Buckle, TN
Date of Birth: Sep 17, 1894
Age: 31y, 3m, 6d.
Color: White - Occupation: At Home
Married
Birthplace: Bedford County, TN
Last place of Residence: Carthage, TN
Husband: Louis Lynch
Father: Arch Woodward
Birthplace: Bedford County, TN
Mother: Eva Foster
Birthplace: Marshall County, TN
Physician: Dr. A.E. Fuston & Dr. Ben L. Burdett

McADAMS, GLENN RUSSELL
Date of Funeral: Aug 10, 1929   2 p.m.
Casket: Flat Top L.S., size 2/6 &Box $ 15.00
Date of Death: Aug 9, 1929 at Home of W.G. McAdams, 25th District,
Bedford County, TN
Place of Funeral: New Herman
Ordered by Mike McAdams, No. 72 First Street, Huntsville, Alabama,
Lowes Mill.
Date of Birth: Oct 31, 1928
Age: 10m, 9 d.
Birthplace: Alabama
Father: Mike McAdams
Birthplace: Bedford County, TN
Mother: Jennie Armstrong
Birthplace: Georgia
Physician: Dr. T.J. Coble

McANALLY, PAUL
Date of Funeral: Mar 15, 1927   4 p.m.
Casket: ____, size 6/0 & Box &
Hearse, Sheets, Fluids, Mattress & etc $ 110.00
Ordered by Mrs. Paul McAnally, 1009 Mansfield Ave., Nashville, TN &
Thos. L. McAnally, Shelbyville, TN
Date of Death: Lock #8 Cumberland River
Place of Funeral: Miss Tishie Martin's house, Shelbyville, TN
Clergyman: Mr. Snoddy
Interred: Willow Mount Cemetery, Shelbyville, TN
Date of Birth: Feb 8, 1903
Age: 23y, 11m, 20d.
Color: White – Occupation: Steam Boat Desk Hand
Married
Birthplace: Nashville, TN
Last place of Residence: Nashville, TN
Father: Thos. L. McAnally
Birthplace: Lawrence County, TN
Mother: Nora Kelly
Birthplace: Hickman County, TN

Physician: Not Any
Cause of Death: Drowning

McCONNELL, JOHN SCOTT
Date of Funeral: Nov 24, 1925   1.p.m.
Embalming $ 20.00
Casket: Oct Blk., size 6/3 &
Box, Hearse, Services, Metal Covers   175.00
Burial Garment: Gents B.C. Suit   25.00
Total: $220.00
Ordered by Miss Nora McConnell
Date of Death: Nov 23, 1925 at Shelbyville, TN
Place of Funeral: Home, Shelbyville, TN
Clergyman: Dr. J.W. Cherry & Dr. S.P. White
Interred: Willow Mount Cemetery, Shelbyville, TN
Date of Birth: Apr 6, 1857
Age: 69 yrs.
Color: White – Occupation: Clerk
Married
Birthplace: Bedford County, TN
Physician: Dr. J.L. Morton

McDONALD, MRS. LIZZIE D. JONES
Date of Funeral: Nov 19, 1929   2:30 p.m.
Embalming $ 20.00
Casket: State – T – Rose, (illegible) Silk, Plush   495.00
Size ¾ Couch, Hearse, Services &
Metal Vault: Clerk   125.00
Burial Garment: Orchid silk   32.50
Grave Lining   6.00
5 Trips. Truck, 1 Trip, Truck driver, & etc   12.50
Total: $696.00
Date of Death: Nov 17, 1929 at Home, Shelbyville, TN
Place of Funeral: Home, Shelbyville, TN
Clergyman: rev. W.C. Creasman & Dr. J.S. Sibley
Interred: Willow Mount Cemetery, Shelbyville, TN
Date of Birth: Oct 10, 1861
Age: 68y, 1m, 7d.
Color: White – Occupation: At Home
Married
Birthplace: Lincoln County, TN
Last place of residence: Shelbyville, TN
Husband: Dr. J.P. McDonald, Sr.
Father: T.D. Jones
Birthplace: TN

Mother: Sarah Kimbrough
Birthplace: Lincoln County, TN
Physician: Dr. T.R. Ray

McELROY, SAM
Date of Funeral: Dec 11, 1927   2 p.m.
Removing Remains from Home, Church & Se4rvices $ 20.00
Metal Box Covers   6.00
Total: $ 26.00
Date of Death: _____
Place of Death: Pro. Hospital, Nashville, TN
Place of Funeral: Church of Christ, Deason, TN
Clergyman: Bro. Clyde Gleaves
Interred: McElroy Cemetery, Private Burial Ground
Date of Birth: _____
Age: ____
Color: White – Occupation: Farmer
Married
Last place of Residence: Bedford County, TN

McFADDEN, HENRY CLAY
Date of Funeral: Feb 20, 1925   2 p.m.
Removing Remains from Trail to home and Cemetery. $ 12.00
Drayage on Box   .50
Total: $ 12.50
No other information.

McFARLAND, MRS. EULA MYRTLE
Date of Funeral: Sep 12, 1927   10:30 a.m.
Embalming $ 20.00
Casket: Oct Steel Gray, plush, size 6/3 &
Box, Hearse, Services   200.00
Burial Garment: Silk Dress   26.50
Hose   2.00
Metal Box Covers   6.00
Grave Lining   3.00
Ambulance   2.50
Total: $ 260.00
Ordered by L.B. McFarland
Date of Death: Sep 10, 1927 at Bedford County Hospital
Place of Funeral: Home, 23rd District, Bedford County, TN
Clergyman: Rev. J.E. Vanse
Interred: Willow Mount Cemetery, Shelbyville, TN
Date of Birth: Jul 29, 1898
Age: 29y, 1m, 12d.

Color: White – Occupation: Housewife
Married
Husband: L.B. McFarland
Birthplace: Bedford County, TN
Father: Taylor Cannon
Birthplace: Bedford County, TN
Mother: Mary Moore
Birthplace: Bedford County, TN
Physician: Dr. T.R. Ray

McGILL, JOHN AARON
Date of Funeral: Jan 31, 1926   2 p.m.
Casket: Sil Gray, B. Couch, size 5/4 &
Hearse, Services $ 350.00
Metal Vault, Style, Clark   125.00
Burial Garment: Gents Suit   35.00
Total: $ 510.00
Ordered by Oscar Sartain
Date of Death: Jan 30, 1926 on 23rd District, Bedford County, TN
Place of Funeral: Home, 23rd District, Bedford County, TN
Interred: Willow Mount Cemetery, Shelbyville, TN
Date of Birth: Nov 1, 1841
Age: 84 yrs.
Color: White – Occupation: Farmer
Married
Physician: Dr. T.J. Coble
No other Information

McGILL, MRS. MARY ELIZABETH
Date of Funeral: Mar 19, 1929   11 a.m.
Casket: Batesville State, ½ Couch, size 6/3 &
Gray Plush, Hearse, Services $ 350.00
Metal Vault, Style, Clark   125.00
Burial Garment: Orchid Silk Dress   30.00
Grave Lining, Hose, Drayage, etc   5.00
Total: $ 510.00
Ordered by Oscar Sartain
Date of Death: Mar 18, 1929 at Home, 23rd District, Bedford County, TN
Place of Funeral: Home, 23rd District, Bedford County, TN
Clergyman: Rev. Clyde Gleaves
Interred: Willow Mount Cemetery, Shelbyville, TN
Date of Birth: Nov 22, 1847
Age: 81y, 3m, 24d.
Color: White – Occupation: At Home
Widow

Birthplace: Bedford County, TN
Husband: Jno. A. McGill (deceased)
Father: Robert Terry
Birthplace: North Carolina
Mother: Elizabeth Bobo
Birthplace: TN
Physician: Dr. T.J. Coble

McGILL, RAYMOND INGLE
Date of Funeral: Jul 28, 1925   10 a.m.
Embalming $ 20.00
Casket: Half Couch, Gray, size 6/3   400.00
Clark Grave Vault   125.00
Grave Lining   3.50
Drayage on Chairs, Vault & to Cemetery   2.50
Total: $551,99
Ordered by W.J. McGill
Date of Death: Jul 27, 1925 at Shelbyville, TN
Place of Funeral: Home, Shelbyville, TN
Clergyman: Dr. Vanse, Dr. Holder & Mr. Tate
Interred: Willow Mount Cemetery, Shelbyville, TN
Date of Birth: Oct 2, 1901
Age: 24yrs.
Color: White – Occupation: Traveling Salesman
Single
Birthplace: Shelbyville, TN
Physician: Dr. Avery

McGREW, DR. SAMUEL J.
Date of Funeral: Jun 21, 1926   10 a.m.
Embalming $ 20.00
Casket: ½ Cough, State Gray, size 6/3 &
Box (Batesville), Hearse, Services   450.00
Grave Lining   2.00
Metal Box Covers   6.00
Drayage & Drivers   3.50
Total: $ 480.00
Date of Death: Jul 19, 1926 at Home, Shelbyville, TN
Place of Funeral: Home, Shelbyville, TN
Clergyman: Dr. Robinson & Dr. Cherry
Interred: Willow Mount Cemetery, Shelbyville, TN
Date of Birth: Dec 11, 1855
Age: ____
Married
Father: Dr. J.H. McGrew

Physician: Dr. T.R. Ray

McGREW, JAMES HENRY
Date of Funeral: Dec 12, 1927   2 p.m.
Embalming: $ 20.00
Casket: Blk. B.C. Cedar, size 6/6 &
Hearse, Services   225.00
Metal Vault, Style: Clark   125.00
White Silk Hose   .75
Grave Lining   6.00
Total: $375.75
Date of Death: Dec 11, 1927 at Home, Shelbyville, TN
Clergyman: Dr. J.S. Sibley
Interred: Willow Mount Cemetery, Shelbyville, TN
Date of Birth: Jul 17, 1853
Age: 74y, 4m, 23d.
Color: White – Occupation: Druggist
Widower
Birthplace: Bedford County, TN
Father: Jos. H. McGrew
Birthplace: Bedford County, TN
Mother: Lattie Cannon
Birthplace: Bedford County, TN
Physician: Dr. H.W. Moody

McLANE, BESSIE RUTH (COL)
Date of Funeral: Nov 8, 1926   2 p.m.
Casket: Flat Top L.S., size 4/6 &
No Hearse or Services $ 37.00
Date of Death: Nov 7, 1926 at 23rd District, Bedford County, TN
Place of Funeral: 23rd District, Bedford County, TN
Interred: Mt. Zion
Date of Birth: ____
Age: 7 yrs.
Color: Colored
Birthplace: Bedford County, TN
Father: Henry McLane
Birthplace: Bedford County, TN
Mother: Fannie Johnson
Birthplace: Bedford County, TN
Physician: Dr. T.J. Coble

McLANE, FANNY JOHNSON
Date of Funeral: Jul __, 1922   12 a.m.
Embalming $ 20.00

Casket: Sil Gray E. Crepe, size 6/3

Box, Hearse, Services	$ 100.00
Burial Garment: White Silk Dress	15.00
Hose	1.00
Metal Box Covers	6.00
Total:	$ 142.00

Ordered by Henry McLane, R-5, Shelbyville, TN
Date of Death: Jul 20, 1928 at 10.p.m.
Place of Death: Home. 25th District, Bedford County, TN
Place of Funeral: Mt. Zion
Interred: Mt. Zion Cemetery
Date of Birth: Jun 23, 1887
Age: 41y, 27d.
Color: Colored – Occupation: Housewife
Married
Birthplace: Bedford County, TN
Husband: Henry McLane
Father: Sam Johnson
Birthplace: Bedford County, TN
Mother: Lou Moore
Birthplace: TN
Physician: Not Any

MARSHALL, L.N.

Date of Funeral: Feb 17, 1925   10 a.m.

Casket: Blk. Eng. Crape, size 6/0 & Box	$ 100.00
Burial Garment: Winding Sheet & Shirt	8.37
Drayage on 3 day chairs & Box	1.00
Metal Box Covers	5.00
Grave Lining	1.50
Total:	$ 115.87

Date of Death: Feb 1, 1925 at Shelbyville, TN
Place of Funeral: Shelbyville, TN
Clergyman: Dr. S.P. White
Interred: Willow Mount Cemetery, Shelbyville, TN
Date of Birth: Mar 6, 1849
Age: 76 yrs.
Color: White
Birthplace: Tullahoma, TN
Last place of Residence: Shelbyville, TN
Physician: Dr. T.R. Ray

MARSHALL, MRS. JULIA

Date of Funeral: Oct 29, 1925
Removing Remains from Nashville, TN &

Casket: Size 6/3, B & Box	$ 60.00

Date of Death: Oct 28, 1925 at Central State Hospital, Nashville, TN
Place of Funeral: Shelbyville, TN
Interred: _____
Date of Birth: ____
Age: 23 yrs.
Color: White
Husband: Bob Marshall
Cause of Death: Broken Hip

MARSHALL, WILLLIAM BURR

Date of Funeral: Nov 15, 1929   10 a.m.

Removing Remains from Depot to

Funeral Home to Cemetery	$ 20.00
Grave Metal Boards	6.00
Grave Lining	3.50
Drayage & Truck	6.50
Total:	$ 36.00

Date of Death: Nov 12, 1929 at Chicago, Illinois
Place of Funeral: Thompson Funeral Home, Shelbyville, TN
Clergyman: Rev. Trotter & Miss Maggie Cox
Interred: Willow Mount Cemetery, Shelbyville, TN
Date of Birth: ____

Age: 68 yrs.
Color: White
Married
No other information

MARTIN, BASIL JR.
Date of Funeral: May 25, 1926   10 a.m.
Casket: White L.S., Flat Top, size 2/0 &
Box, Car, Services $ 15.00
Date of Death: May 25, 1926 at Home, Shelbyville, TN
Place of Funeral: Home, Shelbyville, TN
Interred: Willow Mount Cemetery, Shelbyville, TN
Date of Birth: May 24, 1926
Age: 1 day
Color: White
Birthplace: Shelbyville, TN
Father: Basil Martin
Birthplace: TN
Mother: Ruby Kingston
Birthplace: TN
Physician: Dr. J.L. Morton

MARTIN, JAMES D. JR.
Date of Funeral: Feb 19, 1925   2 p.m.
Casket: White P K, size 3/0 &
Box, Metals, Services $ 32.00
Date of Death: Feb 18, 1925 at Shelbyville, TN
Place of Funeral: Shelbyville, TN
Date of Birth: Sep 25, 1923
Age: 1y, 4m
Color: White
Birthplace: Tullahoma, TN
Father: James D. Martin
Mother: _____
Physician: Dr. Avery

MARTIN, MRS. TENNIE
Date of Funeral: Apr 30, 1925   2 p.m.
Embalming: $ 20.00
Casket: Gray, Plush, size 6/0   175.00
Metal, Box Covers   5.00
Total: $ 200.00
Ordered by Tom Martin
Date of Death: Apr 29, 1925 at Flat Creek, TN
Place of Funeral: New Herman

Date of Birth: _____
Age: 61 yrs.
Widow
Physician: Dr. Conditt

MASSIE, JNO. T.
Date of Funeral: Dec 29, 1925   2 p.m.
Embalming $ 20.00
Casket: Sil Gray, plush, size 6/3 &
Hinge Cap, Box, Hearse, Services   200.00
Metal Box Covers   5.00
Grave Lining   3.00
Total: $ 288.00
Ordered by John Massie & Walter Massie
Date of Death: Dec 28, 1925 at Home, Shelbyville, TN
Place of Funeral: Home, Shelbyville, TN
Clergyman: Dr. S.A. White
Interred: Willow Mount Cemetery, Shelbyville, TN
Date of Birth: Oct 21, 1849
Age: 76 yrs.
Color: White – Occupation: Not Any
Married
Birthplace: North Carolina
Last place of Residence: Shelbyville, TN
Physician: Dr. W.H. Avery

MAUPIN, JOHN (COL)
Date of Funeral: Mar 6, 1929
Casket: B. (County), size 6/3 $ 12.00
Date of Death: Mar 4, 1929 at County Poor Farm
Place of Funeral: County Poor Farm
Interred: County Poor Farm
Ordered by W.G. Daniel, Supt. of Bedford County, TN
Date of Birth: Unknown
Age: About 40 yrs.
Color: Colored – Occupation: Farmer
Single
Birthplace: Unknown
Last place of Residence: County Poor Farm
Father: Unknown
Mother: Unknown
Physician: Dr. T.R. Ray

MAUPIN, MRS. EMMA SHOFNER
Date of Funeral: Jan 5, 1926   2 p.m.

Embalming:	$ 20.00
Casket: Sil. Gray, B.C., size 6/3 &	
Full H.T., Hearse, Services	500.00
Metal Vault, Type: Clark	125.00
Burial Garment: White Silk Dress & Scarf	38.00
Slippers	3.00
Grave Lining	2.00
Total:	$688.00

Ordered by Edward Maupin
Date of Death: Jan 4, 1926 near Shelbyville, TN
Place of Funeral: Home near Shelbyville, TN
Clergyman: Dr. Chas. Armstrong
Interred: Jenkins Chapel Cemetery
Date of Birth: Oct 31, 1864
Age: 62 yrs.
Color: White
Widow
Birthplace: Near Shelbyville, TN
Physician: Dr. G.W. Moody

MEACHAM, MRS. MARY MARGARET
Date of Funeral: Mar 5, 1929   2 p.m.

Embalming	$ 20.00
Casket: White Plush, ½ Couch, size 6/3 Chatt &	
Hearse, Services	265.00
Metal Vault, Style, Clark	125.00
Burial Garment: Grave Lining: White & Flesh Silk Dress	28.00
Grave Lining	7.00
Total:	$ 445.00

Ordered by Tucker Meacham
Date of Death: Mar 4, 1929 at Bedford County Hospital
Burial: Mar 5, 1929
Interred: Willow Mount Cemetery, Shelbyville, TN
Date of Birth: Sep 12, 1902
Age: 26y, 5m, 19d.
Color: White – Occupation: House wife
Married
Birthplace: Bedford County, TN
Husband: ____ Meacham
Father: H.L. Stephens
Birthplace: Bedford County, TN
Mother: Sallie Ann Turrentine
Birthplace: Bedford County, TN
Physician: Dr. Jas. L. Morton

MONTGOMERY, ELIAS GREEN
Date of Funeral: Apr 7, 1926   1:30 p.m.
Casket: Gray Silk plush, size 6/3 &
Box, Embalming, Metal boards, Hearse, Services &
Shirt, Tie $ 325.00
Date of Death: Apr 6, 1926 at Home, 24th District, Bedford County, TN
Place of Funeral: Home, 24th District, Bedford County, TN
Clergyman: Dr. S.P. White
Interred: Pearson Cemetery
Date of Birth: Feb 8, 1847
Age: 78 yrs.
Color: White – Occupation: Farmer
Widower
Birthplace: TN
Father: Silas Montgomery
Birthplace: Virginia
Mother: Mary Roach
Birthplace: Don't Know
Physician: Dr. Conditt

MOONINGHAM, MRS. JENNIE
Date of Funeral: Nov 30, 1928
Casket: Sq. L.S., White, size 6/3 &
Box, Hearse, Dress, Services $ 50.00
No other information

MOORE, CAL (COL)
Date of Funeral: Jan 5, 1927   2 p.m.
Casket: B. Coffin, size 6/3, County $ 12.00
Date of Death: Jan 4, 1927 at County House
Place of Funeral: County House
Interred: County Grave yard
Date of Birth: Don't Know
Age: About 85 yrs.
Color: Colored
Widower
Birthplace: Don't Know
Mother: Don't Know
Physician: Dr. T.R. Ray

MOORE, EUGENE
Date of Funeral: Nov 16, 1928   11 a.m.
Removing Remains, Ambulance $ 5.00
Embalming: $ 20.00
Casket: Oct Gray E. Crape, size 6/3 &

Box, Hearse, Services	$ 125.00
Burial Garment: Suit, Collar, Tie & Shirt	29.00
Underwear, Sox	2.50
Metal Box Covers	6.00
Grace Lining	3.00
Total:	$ 190.00

Lot in Cemetery: $23.44
Date of Death: Nov 15, 1928 at Bedford County Hospital
Place of Funeral: Willow Mount Cemetery, Shelbyville, TN
Clergyman: Rev. Gore
Interred: Willow Mount Cemetery, Shelbyville, TN
Date of Birth: Oct 15, 1906
Age: 22y, 1m.
Color: White – Occupation: Carpenter
Physician: Dr. W.H. Avery

MOORE, MATTIE ANN
Date of Funeral: Apr 20, 1926   2:30 p.m.
Embalming: $ 20.00
Casket: white, ½ Couch, size 6/3 &
Hearse, Services   250.00
Outside Case: Cedar   25.00
Metal Box Covers   5.00
Total: $300.00
Ordered by Mrs. Kate Jones
Date of Death: Apr 18, 1926 at Home, Shelbyville, TN
Clergyman: Dr. J.W. Cherry
Interred: Willow Mount Cemetery, Shelbyville, TN
Date of Birth: Aug 19, 1844
Age: 81 yrs.
Color: White – Occupation: Housewife
Widow
Birthplace: Bedford County, TN
Father: Robert N. Jones
Birthplace: North Carolina
Mother: Elizabeth Holland
Birthplace: Rutherford County, TN
Physician: Dr. T.J. Coble

MORRIS, THOMAAS BROWN
Date of Funeral: May 11, 1926   11 a.m.
Casket: Sil Gray Plush, size 6/3 &
Box, Metal Boards, Suit, Hearse, Services $225.00
Ordered by W.H. Morris
Date of Death: May 11, 1926

Place of Funeral: Shelbyville, TN
Clergyman: Dr. Joel Vanse
Interred: Willow Mount Cemetery, Shelbyville, TN
Date of Birth: Oct 30, 1906
Age: 19 yrs.
Color: White – Occupation: Saddlery
Single
Birthplace: Cherokee County, Alabama
Last place of Residence: Shelbyville, TN
Father: Wm. Morris
Birthplace: Alabama
Mother: Sallie Lambert
Birthplace: Georgia
Physician: Dr. W.H. Avery
Cause of Death: T.B.

MORTON, MANDY (COL)
Date of Funeral: Sep 17, 1928
Casket: B., size 6/3 $ 12.00
Date of Death: Sep 16, 1928 at County Farm
Date of Funeral: County Farm
Interred: County Farm
Date of Birth: Unknown
Age: About 80 yrs.
Color: Colored
Birthplace: Bedford County, TN
Father: Unknown
Mother: Unknown
Ordered by W.S. Daniel, Supt. of County Farm, Bedford County, TN

MULLINS, JAMES MADISON
Date of Funeral: Oct 8, 1925   2:30 p.m.
Embalming $ 20.00
Casket: Sil Gray E. Crape, size 6/3 &
Box, Hearse, Services   125.00
Metal Box Covers   5.00
Total: $150.00
Date of Death: Oct 7, 1925 at Shelbyville, TN
Place of Funeral: New Hermon
Clergyman: Dr. White & Dr. Vanse
Date of Birth: Nov 2, 1854
Age: 71 yrs.
Color: White – Occupation: Farmer
Widower
Physician: Dr. Avery

MULLINS, JAMES MARION
Date of Funeral: Jan 26, 1928   2 p.m.
Embalming $ 20.00
Casket: State Blk. B.C., size 6/3 &
Hearse, Services   300.00
Outside Case: Cedar   35.00
Drayage, Extra Equipment & Service for grave   12.50
Grave Lining   3.00
Metal Box Covers   6.00
Total: $376.50
Date of Death: Jan 25, 1928 at E.C. Huffman, Shelbyville, TN
Place of Funeral: Jenkins Chapel
Clergyman: Dr. S.P. White & Dr. Julian Sibley
Interred: Jenkins Chapel Cemetery
Date of Birth: Nov 11, 1837
Age: 90y, 2m, 15d.
Color: White – Occupation: Retired Farmer
Widower
Birthplace: Marion County, TN
Last place of Residence: Shelbyville, TN
Father: John Mullins
Birthplace: TN
Mother: Elizabeth Bradshaw
Birthplace: Unknown
Physician: Dr. G.W. Moody

MULLINS, MISS MAUDE NORMA
Date of Funeral: Sep 13, 1927   2 p.m.
Removing Remains from Hospital $ 5.00
Embalming   20.00
Casket: Oct White L.S., size 6/3 &
Box, Hearse, Services   125 .00
Burial Garment: Winding Sheet (flesh)   20.00
Metal Box Covers   6.00
Total: $ 176.00
Ordered by Fred Mullins
Date of Death: Sep 12, 1927 at Bedford County Hospital
Place of Funeral: First Christian Church, Shelbyville, TN
Clergyman: Rev. J.E. Vanse
Interred: New Herman
Date of Birth: Nov 23, 1886
Age: 42y, 9m, 20d.
Color: White – Occupation: Milliner
Single
Birthplace: Bedford County, TN

MURDOCK, HIRAM WALACE
Date of Funeral: Jul 11, 1929   10 a.m.
Embalming $ 20.00
Casket: Oct, ½ Couch, Gray plush, size 6/3 &
Box, Hearse, Services   265.00
Grave Lining   6.00
Drayage, hairs, & etc   6.00
Total: $ 303.00
Date of Death: Jul 9, 1929 at near Home, 21st District, Bedford County, TN
Place of Funeral: Center Church
Clergyman: Rev. J.E. Trotter
Date of Burial: Jul 11, 1929
Interred: Lewisburg, TN
Date of Birth: Dec 13, 1913
Age: 15y, 6m, 26d.
Color: White – Occupation: At School
Single
Birthplace: Marshall County, TN
Last place of Residence: Bedford County, TN
Father: Hiram Murdock
Birthplace: Marshall County, TN
Mother: Bell Green
Birthplace: Marshall County, TN
Physician: Not Any
Cause of Death: Struck by Lightning

OUT OFF LINE:
MOORE, Mrs. Mary Etta
Date of Funeral: Nov 24, 1928   2 p.m.
Embalming $ 25.00
Casket: State, ½ Couch, Gray Nat., size 6/3 &
Hearse, Services   250.00
Metal Vault, Style Clark   125.00
Total: $400.00
Date of Death: Nov 22, 1928 at Home, near Cottage Grove, TN
Place of Funeral: Church at Cottage Grove. TN
Interred: Cottage Grove Cemetery
Date of Birth: Oct 24, 1858
Age: 70y, 28d.
Color: white – Occupation: Housewife
Married
Birthplace: Giles County, TN
Last place of Residence: Williamson County, TN
Husband: John Moore
Father: Frederick Batte

Birthplace: Unknown
Mother: Francis Tarpley
Birthplace: Bedford County, TN
Physician: Dr. Robinson

MOORE, MRS. MATTIE TUNE
Date of funeral: Feb 25, 1928   2 p.m.
Embalming $ 20.00
Casket: State Gray Metal, size 6/3 &
Hearse, Services   645.00
Outside Case: Cedar   35.00
Metal Box Covers   6.00
Total: $706.00
Date of Death: Feb 23, 1928 at Home, Wartrace Pike
Place of Funeral: Home, Wartrace Pike
Clergyman: Rev. J.W. Cherry & Dr. Sibley
Interred: Jenkins Chapel
Date of Birth: Han 27, 1849
Age: 79y, 27 d.
Color: White – Occupation: House wife
Widow
Birthplace: Bedford County, TN
Husband: Arch Moore (Deceased)
Father: William Tune
Birthplace: Virginia
Mother: Christine Morton
Birthplace: Bedford County, TN
Physician: Dr. T.R. Ray

NANCE, CLEM (Est.)
Date of Funeral: Dec 30, 1924   1 p.m.
Removing Remains from Home to Shelbyville $ 5.00
Casket: Blk Eng Crape, size 6/3   115.00
Suit Cloths   15.00
Metal Box Covers   5.00
Total: $140.00
Ordered by J.T. Cartwright, admr. of Clem Nance Estate
Date of Death: Dec 29, 1924 at Bedford County, TN
Place of Burial: Parsons Grave Yard
Clergyman: Not Any
Date of Birth: Dec 29, 1840
Age: 84 yrs.
Color: White –Occupation: Mechanic
Single
Birthplace: Rutherford County, TN
Last place of Residence: Bedford County, TN
Cause of Death: Found dead in bed.

NANCE, MRS. MOLLIE
Date of Funeral: Nov, 12, 1924   3 p.m.
Casket: 8260, size 6/3 &
Nat C. Co. $ 225.00
Metal Vault, Style, Clerk   125.00
Grave Lining: 1.50
Total: $ 351.50
Ordered by A.R. Nance – A.R. Nance & Sons
Date of Death: Nov 20, 1924 at Shelbyville, TN
Place of Funeral: Shelbyville, TN
Clergyman: Dr. J.W. Cherry & Dr. J.P. Robinson
Interred: Willow Mount Cemetery, Shelbyville, TN
Date of Birth: Nov 19, 1856
Age: 68 yrs.
Color: White – Occupation: Housewife
Married
Birthplace: Shelbyville, TN
Husband: A.R.Nance

Father: Geo. W. Thompson
Birthplace: America
Physician: Dr. Ben Burdett

NEAL, MRS. IRENE
Date of Funeral: Jun 18, 1928   11:30 a.m.
Removing Remains from Depot to Hats Chapel $ 20.00
Metal Box Covers   6.00
Total: $ 26.00
Ordered by Archie Neal, 802 Lawrence Ave., Toledo, Ohio
Date of Death: Jun 16, 1928 at Toledo, Ohio
Place of Funeral: Harts Chapel, Bedford County, TN
Clergyman: Rev. Keathley
Interred: Harts Chapel Cemetery
Date of Birth: Sep 4, 1906
Color: White – Occupation: Housewife
Married
Birthplace: Bedford County, TN
Last Place of Residence: Toledo, Ohio
Husband: Archie Neal
Father: Walter Overcast
Birthplace: Bedford County, TN
Mother: ____
Cause of Death: Cerebro Spinal Meningitis

NEELY, JESSIE THOMAS
Date of Funeral: Dec 13, 1927   10 a.m.
Casket: White L.S., flat Top, size 2/0 & Box $ 12.00
Ordered by Thomas Neely
Date of Death: Dec 12, 1927 at Home, 18th District, Bedford County, TN
Interred: Crowells Grave Yard
Date of Birth: Dec 12, 1927
Age: 0 yr.
Color: White
Birthplace: Bedford County, TN
Father: Thomas Neely
Birthplace: Bedford County, TN
Mother: Louise Stephens
Birthplace: Bedford County, TN

NEELY, MISS ELIZABETH JANE
Date of Funeral: Aug 29, 1927   3 p.m.
Embalming: $ 20.00
Casket: Sil Gray, Oct plush, size 6/3 &
Hearse, Services $ 200.00

Metal Vault, Style Clark	$ 125.00
Burial Garment: Gray Silk Dress	28.00
Slippers	4.00
Total:	$ 377.00

Ordered by Amous(Amos) Brown & Jordan Sanders
Date of Death: Aug 28 1927 at 20th District of Bedford County, TN
Place of Funeral: Big Spring Church
Clergyman: Bro. Crawford & Bro. J.W. Cherry
Interred: Family Burying Place (Gordon Sanders Farm)
Date of Birth: Jun 28, 1942
Age: 85 yrs.
Color: White – Occupation: Housewife
Single
Birthplace: Bedford County, TN
Father: Samuel Neely
Birthplace: TN
Mother: Mary Cunningham
Birthplace: Unknown
Physician: Dr. Jas. L. Morton

NEELY, MRS. JNO. S.
Date of Funeral: Nov 16, 1926   11 a.m.
Casket: Blk E Crape, size 6/3 Chatt &
Box, Hearse, Services $100.00
Date of Death: Nov 15, 1926 at 18th District, Bedford County, TN
Place of Funeral: Mt. Lebanon Church
Clergyman: Dr. Robinson
Interred: Mt. Lebanon, TN
Date of Birth: Aug 4, 1884
Age: 42 yrs.
Color: White – Occupation: Housewife
Married
Birthplace: Bedford County, TN
Husband: Jno. S. Neely
Father: J.H. Darnell
Birthplace: Bedford County, TN
Mother: Emily Cook
Birthplace: Lincoln County, TN
Physician: Dr. J.E. Bias

NEIL, JAMES H.
Date of Funeral: Jan 26, 1925   3 p.m.
Removal Remains from Train $ 15.00
Metal Grave Covers   5.00
Drayage on Box   .50

| Grave Lining | $ 1.50 |
| Total: | $ 22.00 |

Ordered by Miss Alice Burdett
Date of Death: Jan 25, 1925 at Scottsville, Kentucky
Place of Funeral: M.E. Church, Shelbyville, TN
Clergyman: J.W. Cherry
Interred: Willow Mount Cemetery, Shelbyville, TN

NELSON, JOHN THOMAS

Date of Funeral: Aug 15, 1925   1 p.m.
Casket: Blk E. Crape, size 5/4 &
Box, Services & Robe $ 80.00
Ordered by Allie (or Ollie) Nelson, .H. Smith Bible Class, Agnes L. Whiteside Chapter
C.U.D.C.
Date of Death: Aug 14, 1925 at Home
Clergyman: Dr. J. Robinson
Interred: Willow Mount Cemetery, Shelbyville, TN
Date of Birth: Apr 11, 1842
Age: 83 yrs.
Color: White
Widower
Birthplace: TN
Last place of Residence: Shelbyville, TN
Physician: Dr. J.L. Morton

NELSON, MRS. KATE

Date of Funeral: Mar 2, 1928   2 p.m.
Casket: Oct Blk E. Crape, size 5/9 &

Box, Hearse, Services	$ 100.00
Burial Garment: Blk Dress	15.00
Metal Box Covers	6.00
Grave Lining	3.00
Total:	$ 124.00

Date of Death: Mar 1, 1928 at Home, Shelbyville, TN
Clergyman: Dr. Sibley
Interred: Willow Mount Cemetery, Shelbyville, TN
Date of Birth: Feb 20, 1874
Age: 54y, 1m, 9d.
Color: White – Occupation: Housewife
Married
Birthplace: Bedford County, TN
Husband: Ollie Nelson
Father: Clark
Birthplace: Unknown
Mother: Victoria Hamlin

Birthplace: Bedford County, TN
Physician: Dr. T.J. Coble

NEWTON, ERNEST D.
Date of Funeral: Jul 6, 1929   10 a.m.
Removing Remains from Wartrace to Shelbyville, to: home of A.H. Ruth,
To Cemetery $ 25.00
Metal Vault, Style, Clark   125.00
Grave Lining   6.00
Tuc(?), Drayage & etc   5.00
Total: 161.00
Date of Death: Jul 3, 1919 at near Harrisburg, Virginia
Place of Funeral: Willow Mount Cemetery, Shelbyville, TN
Clergyman: Dr. J.S. Sibley
Date of Birth: ____
Age: About 62 yrs.
Color: White – Occupation: Traveling Salesman
Married
Birthplace: TN
No other information.

NICHOLSON, YORK POITEVENT, JR.
Date of Funeral: Nov 29, 1928   3:30 p.m.
Removing Remains from Cornersville, TN to Shelbyville, TN $ 25.00
Metal Vault, Style, Clark   125.00
Inc., Chairs, Tent   3.50
Grave Lining   6.00
Total: $ 159.5
Date of Death: Nov 27, 1929 at New Orleans, Louisiana
Place of Funeral: Willow Mount Cemetery, Shelbyville, TN
Interred: Willow Mount Cemetery, Shelbyville, TN
Date of Birth: ____
Age: 7y, 8m, 14d.
Father: York Nicholson
Birthplace: ____
Mother: Dovie Boyd
Birthplace: Shelbyville, TN

NOBLETT, MANNON GORDON
Date of Funeral: Mar 10, 1928   2.p.m.
Embalming: $ 20.00
Casket: Oct Gray Crape, size 6/3 &
Box, Hearse, Services   125.00
Metal Box Covers   6.00
Shirt, Collar   1.75

Total: $ 152.75
Date of Death: Mar 9, 1928 at 22nd District, Bedford County, TN
Place of Funeral: New Herman
Clergyman: Bro. Largen
Interred: New Herman Cemetery
Date of Birth: Nov 19, 1850
Age: 77y, 3m, 19d.
Color: White – Occupation: Farmer
Married
Birthplace: Bedford County, TN
Farther: John Noblett
Birthplace: Bedford County, TN
Mother: Polly Roser
Birthplace: Unknown
Physician: Dr. T.J. Coble

NOBLETT, MRS. ALICE IRENE
Date of Funeral: Nov 18, 1926   2 p.m.
Casket: White, Lambskin, size 6/3 &
Hearse, Services $ 85.00
Burial Garment: Robe   6.00
Total: 91.00
Date of Death: Nov 17, 1926 at Shelbyville, TN
Clergyman: rev. S.A. Jones
Interred: Shelbyville, TN
Date of Birth: Sep 22, 1902
Age: 24 yrs.
Color White – Occupation: Housewife
Married
Birthplace: TN
Husband: Roy Noblett
Father: A.J. Hamilton
Birthplace: TN
Mother: Ella Charles
Birthplace: TN
Physician: Dr. Jas. L. Morton

NOLEN, MRS. SARAH ANN
Date of Funeral: Dec 22, 1929   2 p.m.
Casket: County Coffin, size 6/3 $ 12.00
Date of Death: Dec 14, 1929 at County Farm
Place of Funeral: County Farm
Interred: County Farm
Date of Birth: Unknown
Age: 84yrs. (about)

Color: White – Occupation: At Home
Widow
No other information

O'NEAL, VIRGINIA ARLINE
Date of Funeral: Dec 18, 1924   1 p.m.
Casket: White, P.K., size 2/0 $ 20.00
Date of Death: Dec 17, 1924 at Hawthorn, TN
Clergyman: Bro. Jess Hart
Interred: Mt. Herman
Date of Birth: Dec 15, 1924
Age: __
Color: White
Single
Birthplace: Hawthron, TN
Father: Dewey Franklin O'Neal
Mother: John (?) Nealy O'Neal
Physician: Dr. Fuston

ODUM, MRS. CORINNE
Date of Funeral: Apr 21, 1929   2 p.m.
Embalming $ 20.00
Casket: Oct White L.S., size 6/3 &
Box; Hearse, Services   140.00
Burial Garment: White Silk Dress   27.00
Grave Lining   3.00
Metal Box Covers   6.00
Total: $ 196.00
Date of Death: Apr 19, 1929 at Bedford County Hospital
Place of Funeral: Home, Mrs. Stateman (?)
Interred: Willow Mount Cemetery, Shelbyville, TN
Date of Birth: Oct 18, 1910
Age: 18y, 6m, 2d.
Color: White – Occupation: Mill Hand
Married
Father: Walter Bell
Birthplace: Bedford County, TN
Mother: Maynor Little
Birthplace: Rutherford County, TN
Physician: Dr. Jas. L. Morton

OLIVER, JAMES
Date of Funeral: Jan 26, 1929   11 a.m.
Casket: Flay Top L.S., size 2/0 & Box $ 12.50
Date of Death: Jan 25, 1929 at Home, Shelbyville, TN
Interred: Center Cemetery
Date of Birth: Jan 25, 1929
Age: 0y, Stillborn
Birthplace: Bedford County, TN

Father: John Olliver
Birthplace: Marshall County, TN
Mother: Gertie Elliott
Birthplace: Bedford County, TN
Physician: Dr. W.H. Avery

OLLIVER, WILLIAM
Date of Funeral: Feb 10, 1929   1:30 p.m.
Casket: Oct White L.S., size 3/0 &
Box, Hearse, Services, Metals $ 59.50
Date of Death: Feb 9, 1928 at Home, Shelbyville Mills, TN
Place of Funeral: Home, Shelbyville Mills, TN
Clergyman: Rev. E.P. Watson
Interred at Center Cemetery
Date of Birth: Mar 28, 1928
Age: 1y, 10m, 12d.
Color: White
Birthplace: Alabama
Last place of Residence: Bedford County, TN
Father: John Oliver
Birthplace: Marshall County, TN
Mother: Gertie Elliott
Birthplace: Bedford County, TN
Physician: Dr. W.H. Avery

PAINTER, JAMES RUFUS
Date of Funeral: Dec 21, 1926   2 p.m.
Casket: White, L.S., Flat Top, size 2/0 &
Box, Car, Services $ 20.00
Date of Death: Dec 20, 1926 at Home, Shelbyville, TN
Place of Funeral: Home, Shelbyville, TN
Interred: Willow Mount Cemetery, Shelbyville, TN
Date of Birth: Aug 31, 1926
Age: 4m, 20d.
Color: White
Birthplace: Bedford County, TN
Father: R.F. Painter
Birthplace: Bedford County, TN
Mother: Liza Tucker
Birthplace: Moore County, TN
Physician: Dr. as. L. Morton

PALMER, MRS. MIGNONETTE
Date of Funeral: Dec 31, 1929   10:30 a.m.
Embalming $ 20.00

Casket: State Gray, ½ couch, Batesville &
Hearse, Services $ 340.00
Metal Vault, Style, Clark   125.00
Burial Garment: Silk Dress   30.00
Funeral Notice   xxxx
Grave Lining   6.00
Drayage, Chairs   4.00
Total: $ 325.00
Ordered by Fred Walker
Date of Death: Dec 30, 1929 at Home, Shelbyville, TN
Place of Funeral: Home, Shelbyville, TN
Clergyman: Rev. W.E. Doss
Interred: Willow Mount Cemetery, Shelbyville, TN
Date of Birth: Aug 28, 1881
Age: 48y, 4m, 3d.
Color: White – Occupation: At Home
Widow
Birthplace: Marshall County, TN
Last place of Residence: Bedford County, TN
Husband: Ed Palmer
Father: J.M. Anderson
Birthplace: Marshall County, TN
Mother: Amanda M. Erwin
Birthplace: Marshall County, TN
Physician: Dr. Ben L. Burdett

PALMER, WILLIAM EDWIN
Date of Funeral: Jul 6, 1929   2:30 p.m.
Embalming: $ 20.00
Casket: Gray State, ½ Couch, Batesville, size 6/3 &
Hearse, Services   373.00
Metal Vault, Style, Clark   125.00
Ambulance   xxxx
Grave Lining   3.00
Drayage, etc.   4.00
Total: $ 525.00
Date of Death: Jul 5, 1929 at Vanderbilt Hospital, Nashville, TN
Place of Funeral: Home, Shelbyville, TN
Clergyman: Rev. J.W. Cherry & Rev. W.E. Doss
Interred: Willow Mount Cemetery, Shelbyville, TN
Date of Birth: Dec 17, 1876
Age: 53y, 6m, 18d.
Color: White – Occupation: Mill Supt.
Married
Birthplace: Marshall County, TN

Last place of Residence: Shelbyville, TN
Father: Robert Palmer
Birthplace: Virginia
Mother: Rebecca Pigg
Birthplace: TN
Physician: Dr. Ben L. Burdett & C.M. Smith, Vanderbilt, Nashville, TN

PARKER, ELANOR JEAN
Date of Funeral: Nov 30, 1923   10 a.m.
Embalming $ 15.00
Casket: White plush, size 3/0 &
Box, Couch, Personal Service   125.00
Metal Box Covers   5.00
Grave Lining   2.00
Total: $ 147.00
Ordered by Dan Parker
Date of Death: Nov 29, 1925 at Hospital, Shelbyville, TN
Place of Funeral: Cemetery, Shelbyville, TN
Clergyman: Dr. J.W. Cherry & E.P. Watson
Interred: Willow Mount Cemetery, Shelbyville, TN
Date of Birth: Jun 9, 1925
Age: 5m.
Color: White
Birthplace: Hospital, Shelbyville, TN
Father: Dan Parker
Mother: Ella Parker
Physician: Dr. Coble

PARKER, JOSEPH G., JR.
Date of Funeral: Dec 6, 1928   1:30 p.m.
Casket: ½ couch, State Gray, Batesville &
Hearse, Services, Clark Vault, Suit clothes, Slippers $ 490.00
Date of Death: Dec 5, 1928 at Home, Joe Parker, Jr., 20th District of
Bedford County, TN
Place of Funeral: Flat Creek Baptist Church
Clergyman: Rev. Geo. Gowan
Interred: Flat Creek, TN
Date of Birth: Feb 14, 1852
Age: 76y, 9m, 21d.
Color: White – Occupation: Farmer
Widower
Birthplace: Bedford County, TN
Father: J.G. Parker
Birthplace: North Carolina
Mother: ____ Howard

Physician: Dr. Ben L. Burdett

PARKER, SARAH ANN
Date of Funeral: Nov 14, 1926   2 p.m.
Casket: State Sil Gray, size 6/3 &
Chatt, Hearse, Personal Service $ 300.00
Metal Vault, Style, Clark   125.00
Burial Garment: White Silk Dress   30.50
Slippers   4.50
Silk Hose   2.00
Total: $ 462.00
Date of Death: Nov 13, 1926 at Hospital, Shelbyville, TN
Place of Funeral: Baptist Church, Flat Creek, TN
Clergyman: Dr. Geo. Gowan
Interred: Flat Creek Cemetery
Date of Birth: Feb 17, 1861
Age: 61yrs.
Color: White – Occupation: Housewife
Married
Birthplace: Bedford County, TN
Husband: Joe Parker
Father: Marion Ray
Birthplace: TN
Mother: Don't Know
Physician: Dr. T.J. Coble

PARKES, MISS LANIA MOORE
Date of Funeral: _____
Removing Remains from Hospital $ 5.00
Embalming   20.00
Burial Garment: Winding Sheet   18.00
Slippers   3.50
Hearse   10.00
Ambulance from Hospital   5.00
Total: $ 56.50
Ordered by Thos. L. Bobo
Date of Death: Feb 3, 1927 at Bedford County Hospital, Shelbyville, TN
Place of Funeral: Home near Lynchburg, TN
Interred: Lynchburg, TN
Date of Birth: Apr 21, 1873
Age: 53 yrs.
Color: White – Single
Birthplace: Moore County, TN
Father: Albert H. Parker
Birthplace: TN

Mother: Elizabeth Keller(?)
Birthplace: Illinois
Physician: Dr. Ben Burdett

PARSON, FRED (COL)
Date of Funeral: Nov 29, 1924

Embalming:	$ 15.00
Casket: B & Box, size 6/3	25.00
Burial Garment: Mans Robe	5.00
Hearse	5.00
Total:	$ 50.00

Date of Death: Nov 26, 1924 at Bedford County Hospital
Place of Funeral: Selbyville, TN
Interred: Colored Cemetery, Shelbyville, TN
Date of Birth: Apr 29, 1905
Age: 19 yrs.
Color: Black – Occupation: Farmer
Married
Birthplace: Bedford County, TN
Physician: Dr. Coble
Cause of Death: Automobile Accident

PARSONS, MRS. MARY JEAN BUTTS
Date of Funeral: Sep 25, 2929   2 p.m.

Embalming	$ 20.00
Casket, Oct Gray, ½ couch, size 6/3 &	
Box, Hearse, Services	265.00
Burial Garment: Silk Dress	30.00
Underwear, Hose, etc.	3.75
Grave Lining	3.00
Ambulance	3.00
Drayage, etc	5.00
Total:	$329.75

Date of Death: Sep 24, 1929 at Bedford County Hospital, Shelbyville, TN
Place of Funeral: Methodist Church, South, Shelbyville, TN
Clergyman: Rev. W.E. Doss & J.E. Trotter
Interred: Willow Mount Cemetery, Shelbyville, TN
Date of Birth: Apr 19, 1899
Age: 31y, 5m, 5d.
Married
Birthplace: Bedford County, TN
Husband: Sam Bell Parsons
Father: Joe F. Batts
Birthplace: Bedford County, TN

Mother: Anna Tune
Birthplace: Bedford County, TN
Physician: Dr. Ben L. Burdett & Dr. T.J. Coble

PARSONS, MRS. SALLIE MOULDER
Date of Funeral: Dec 9, 1929   2 p.m.
Casket: State solid (..?), size 6/3 &
Box Metals, Winding Sheet, Hearse, Sox $ 215.00
Date of Death: Dec 8, 1929 at Home, 11th District, Bedford County, TN
Place of Funeral: Crowell Chapel
Clergyman: Rev. Chas. Armstrong
Interred: Crowell Chapel Cemetery
Date of Birth: Nov 25, 1859
Age: 70y, 12d.
Color: White – Occupation: At Home
Widow
Birthplace: TN
Husband: Geo. Parsons
Father: Jasper Moulder
Birthplace: TN
Mother: Sarah Jane Delk
Birthplace: TN
Physician: Dr. W.H. Avery

PARSONS, VOLNEY STRICKLAND
Date of Funeral: Nov 17, 1926   2:30 p.m.
Removing Remains from Hospital $ 3.00
Embalming   20.00
Casket: State 8262, Gray, size 6/3 &
Hearse, Services   325.00
Metal Vault, Style, Clark   125.00
Burial Garment: Suit, Shirt, Collar   28.50
Hose   .75
Grave Lining   2.00
Underwear   2.00
Total: $ 506.25
Date of Death: Nov 15, 1926 at Hospital, Shelbyville, TN 6:30 a.m.
Place of Funeral: M.E. Church, Shelbyville, TN
Clergyman: Dr. J.W. Cherry
Date of Birth: Feb 23, 1852
Age: 74 yrs.
Color: White – Occupation: Banker
Birthplace: Bedford County, TN
Father: Geo. W. Parsons
Birthplace: ____

Mother: Betsy Allison
Birthplace: ____
Physician: Dr. Jas. L. Morton

PEACOCK, MRS. SARAH JANE
Date of Funeral: Mar 12, 1929   2:30 p.m.
Casket: Oct Blk, B.C., Cedar, size 6/0 &
Hearse, Services $ 175.00
Metal Box Covers   6.00
Grave Lining   3.00
Drayage, etc   3.50
Total: $ 187.50
Date of Death: Mar 11, 1928 at Home, 6th District, Bedford County, TN
Place of Funeral: Mrs. Eugene Blakemore, Shelbyville, TN
Clergyman: Dr. Julian Sibley
Interred: Willow Mount Cemetery, Shelbyville, TN
Date of Birth: Feb 6, 1835
Age: 90, 1m, 5d.
Color: White – Occupation: Housewife
Widow
Birthplace: Bedford County, TN
Husband: Marcus Peacock
Father: Dr. Thomas Lipscomb
Birthplace: Virginia
Mother: Rebecca Stephens
Birthplace: Ireland
Physician: Dr. Jas. L. Morton

PHILLIPS, MRS. MARY ETTA
Date of Funeral: Apr 6, 1926   2 p.m.
Casket: White P.K., size 6/3 &
Box, Hearse, Services $ 125.00
Burial Garment: Silk Dress   26.00
Metal Box Covers   5.00
Total: $ 150.00
Ordered by G.M. Phillips & J.D. Phillips
Date of Death: Apr 5, 1926 at Home, Shelbyville, TN
Place of Funeral: Home, Shelbyville, TN
Clergyman: Dr. Cherry & Dr. Keathly
Interred: Wartrace, TN
Date of Birth: Sep 23, 1857
Age: 68 yrs.
Color: White – Occupation: Housewife
Married
Last place of Residence, Shelbyville, TN

Father: Mitchell Cully
Mother: _____
Physician: Dr. W.H. Avery

PHILIPS, DONN CARLOS
Date of Funeral: Sep 7, 1927   2:30 p.m.
Embalming $ 20.00
Casket: Oct Sil Gray, plush, size 6/3 &
Box, ½ couch, Hearse, Services   160.00
Burial Garment: Underwear, Sox, Tie   5.00
Metal Box Covers   6.00
Ambulance removing body   4.00
Total: $ 196.00
Ordered by Blanch Phillips
Date of Death: Sep 5, 1927 at Bedford County Hospital
Clergyman: Bro. Chas. Armstrong
Interred: Horse Mt. Cemetery
Date of Birth: Apr 22, 1873
Age: 54y, 4m, 14d.
Married
Birthplace: Bedford County, TN
Father: Arch Phillips
Birthplace: Bedford County, TN
Mother: Tabitha Shriver
Birthplace: Bedford County, TN
Physician: Dr. T.J. Coble

PHILLIPS, MARVIN MOORE
Date of Funeral: May 13, 1927   2 p.m.
Casket: White, plush, size 3/0 & Box $ 25.00
Date of Death: May 12, 1927 at Home, 3rd District, Bedford County, TN
Place of Funeral: Horse Mt., Bedford County, TN
Clergyman: Bro. Keathley
Interred: Horse Mt. Cemetery
Date of Birth: Nov 15, 1925
Age: 1y, 6m.
Color: White
Birthplace: Bedford County, TN
Father: D.C. Phillips
Birthplace: Bedford County, TN
Mother: Blanch Purdy
Birthplace: Bedford County, TN
Physician: Dr. T.J. Coble

PHILLIPS, MRS. BERTHA ELIZABETH
Date of Funeral: Sep 3, 1929   2 p.m.
Embalming $ 20.00
Casket: Oct Gray, plush, size 6/3 &
Box, Hearse, Services   200.00
Metal Box Covers   5.00
Grave Lining, Truck, etc.   10.00
Flowers $10.00
Total: $235.00
Date of Death: Sep 2, 1929 at Home, 3rd District Bedford County, TN
Place of Funeral: Methodist Church, Wartrace, TN
Clergyman: Rev. Roberts & Croslin
Interred: Hollywood Cemetery, Wartrace, TN
Date of Birth: Nov 28, 1903
Age: 25y, 9m, 4d.
Color: White – Occupation: At Home
Married
Birthplace: Bedford County, TN
Husband: Walter Phillips
Father: Chas. D. Osteen
Birthplace: Bedford County, TN
Mother: Bettie Covington
Birthplace: Marshall County, TN
Physician: Dr. M.L. Connell

PHILLIPS, SAMUEL EVERETT
Date of Funeral: Aug 18, 1929   11 a.m.
Embalming $ 20.00
Casket: ct, ½ couch, Gray Plush, size 6/3 &
Box, Hearse, Services   265.00
Burial Garment: Suit, Collar, Tie, Shirt &
Hose, Underwear   30.00
Metal Box Covers   5.00
Total: $320.00
Date of Death: Aug 15, 1929 at Home, Raby (?), 20th District, Bedford Co., TN
Place of Funeral: Horse Mt.
Interred: Horse Mt., Cemetery, Bedford County, TN
Birthplace: Dec 10, 1859
Age: 69y, 8m, 5d.
Color: White – Occupation: Farmer
Widower
Birthplace: Bedford County, TN
Father: Geo. Phillips
Birthplace: Bedford County, TN
Mother: Elisa Chambers

Birthplace: Bedford County, TN
Physician: Dr. T.R. Ray

PHILPOT, WILLLIAM ALLEN
Date of Funeral: Nov 17, 1926   11 a.m
Casket: Sil Gray, plush, size 6/3 &
Box, Hearse, Metals, Services $ 20.00
1 Shirt, Tie, Sox   2.75
Total: $202.75
Date of Death: Nov 16, 1926 at 4th District, Bedford County, TN
Place of Funeral: Himesville, Bedford County, TN
Clergyman: ___ Jones
Interred: New Hope Cemetery, Bedford County, TN
Date of Birth: Apr 2, 2836
Age: 90 yrs.
Color: White – Occupation: Farmer
Widower
Birthplace: Bedford County, TN
Father: Chas. Philpot
Birthplace: Virginia
Mother: Rebecca Hix
Birthplace: TN
Physician: Dr. Moon

PHILPOTT, MRS. MARY LOU JANE
Date of Funeral: Oct 17, 1929   2 p.m.
Casket: Oct Whit e, plush. ½ couch, size 6/3 &
Winding Sheet, Hearse, Services, Metals $ 250.00
       Flowers: $5.00
Date of Death: Oct 16, 1929 at Home, Bedford County, TN
Place of Funeral: Home, Bedford County, TN
Clergyman: Rev.(illegible) & Short
Interred: Willow Mount Cemetery, Shelbyville, TN
Date of Birth: Aug 10, 1868
Age: 61y, 2m, 6d.
Color: White – Occupation: At Home
Married
Birthplace: Bedford County, TN
Husband: David Philpot
Father: Reed
Birthplace: Bedford County, TN
Mother: Jane McFarland
Birthplace: Bedford County, TN
Physician: Dr. Ben L. Burdett

PIERCE, MRS. BESSIE NOBLETT
Date of Funeral: Jul 10, 1928   10 a.m.

Embalming	$ 20.00
Casket: Oct White, ½ couch, size 6/3 &	
Box, Hearse, Services	265.00
Burial Garment: Silk Dress	33.00
Metal Box Covers	6.00
Hose (Silk)	2.00
Slippers	4.00
Total:	$ 330.00

Ordered by Ross Pierce
Date of Death: Jul 9, `918 at Home, 20th District, Bedford County, TN
Place of Funeral: New Herman
Clergyman: Rev. Frank Tinder
Interred: New Herman Cemetery
Date of Birth: Sep 17, 1891
Age: 36y, 9m, 2d.
Color: White – Occupation: Housewife
Birthplace: Bedford County, TN
Husband: Ross Pierce
Father: Jno. Noblett
Birthplace: Bedford County, TN
Mother: Nary Bartlett
Birthplace: Bedford County, TN
Physician: Dr. Ben Burdett

PILKINGTON, (Infant of Claude Pilkington)
Date of Funeral: Oct 13, 1927   1 p.m.

Casket: Flat Top L.S., size 2/0 &	
Box, Services	$ 20.00

Date of Death: Oct 13, 1927 at Home, Shelbyville, TN
Place of Funeral: Home, Shelbyville, TN
Interred: Willow Mount Cemetery, Shelbyville, TN
Date of Birth: Oct 13, 1927
Stillborn
Color: White
Birthplace: Shelbyville, TN
Father: laude Pilkington
Birthplace: Bedford County, TN
Mother: Lula Irene Pilkington
Birthplace: Rutherford County, TN
Physician: Dr. Jas. L. Morton

PILKINGTON, SIDNEY RUFUS
Date of Funeral: Nov 10, 1929

Casket: Sq. Flat Top, Gray, Crape &
Box, Hearse, Services, Robe $ 75.00
Date of Death: Nov 9, 1929 at Bedford County Hospital, Shelbyville, TN
Place of Funeral: Beech Grove, TN
Interred: Chadwick Grave Yard, near Beech Grove, TN
Date of Birth: May 25, 1856
Age: 73y, 5m, 15d.
Color: White – Occupation: Farmer
Married
Birthplace: Rutherford County, TN
Last place of Residence: Shelbyville, TN
Father: Wm. Pilkington
Physician: Dr. Jas. L. Morton

POARCH, DAUATHY SYBLE
Date of Funeral: Jan 1, 1928   2 p.m.
Casket: County Coffin, size 2/0 $ 6.00
Date of Death: Jan 1, 1928 at Home, Shelbyville, TN
Place of Funeral: Home, Shelbyville, TN
Clergyman: C.M. Thompson
Interred: Willow Mount Cemetery, Shelbyville, TN
Date of Birth: Sep 1, 1927
Age: 4m, 0d.
Birthplace: Marshall County, TN
Last place of residence: Shelbyville, TN
Father: Golie Poarch
Birthplace: Lincoln County, TN
Mother: Lilly Bough
Birthplace: Marshall County, TN
Physician: Dr. W.H. Avery

POPE, BLANCHIE
Date of Funeral: Jul 2, 1928
Casket: Flat Top, L.S., size 3/0 &
Box, Ambulance $ 30.00
Ordered by Mrs. A.A. Pope
Date of Death: July 1, 1928 at Bedford County Hospital, Shelbyville, TN
Place of Funeral: Rutherford County, TN
Interred: Pope Grave Yard
Date of Birth: Feb 7, 1927
Age: 1y, 4m, 23d.
Color: White
Birthplace: Bedford County, TN
Father: Arch Pope
Birthplace: Rutherford County, TN

Mother: Flora Windrow
Birthplace: Rutherford County, TN
Physician: Dr. Jas. L. Morton

POTTS, ALBERT LEE
Date of Funeral: Nov 18, 1927   2 p.m.
Casket: Oct White, L.S., size 3/6
Box, Metals: $ 39.00
Date of Death: Nov 17, 1927 at Home of Mrs. Marcus Potts
Place of Funeral: Home of Mrs. Marcus Potts
Interred: Pressgrove Grave Yard
Date of Birth: Oct 9, 1925
Age: 2y, 1m, 8 d.
Color: White
Birthplace: Bedford County, TN
Father: Cartwright Potts
Birthplace: Bedford County, TN
Mother: Robie Lee Sudberry
Birthplace: Bedford County, TN
Physician: Dr. Jno. Garrett, Rock Vale, TN

POTTS, ELISHA H.
Date of Funeral: Aug 13, 1926   11 a.m.
Removing Remains, Ambulance from Hospital to Home, Metal Box Covers &
Underwear, Sox &
Casket: Chatt. State, size 6/3 &
Box, Hearse, Services, Suit, Shirt, Tie $ 375.00
Date of Death: Aug 11, 1926 at Hospital, Shelbyville, TN
Place of Funeral: Zion Hill
Clergyman: Dr. Keathley
Interred: Mt. Zion Cemetery
Date of Birth: Jun 10, 1859
Age: 67yrs
Color: White – Occupation: Farmer
Widower
Birthplace: Bedford County, TN
Father: Cartwright Pott
Birthplace: Don't Know
Mother: ____ Jackson
Birthplace: TN
Physician: Dr. T.J. Coble

POTTS, MARCUS LAFAYETTE
Date of Funeral: Jun 27, 1927   11 a.m.
Embalming $ 20.00

Casket: Oct Blk, B.C., size 6/3 $ 150.00
Box, Hearse, Services, Burial Garment: Blk B.C. Suit   20.00
Total: $ 190.00
Date of Death: Jun 26, 1927 at Home, 11th District, Bedford County, TN
Place of Funeral: Maxwell Chapel
Clergyman: Rev. Kerney & Rev. Keathley
Interred: Pressgrove Grave Yard
Date of Birth: Jan 2, 1857
Age: 70y. 5m, 24d.
Married
Birthplace: Bedford County, TN
Father: A.C. Potts
Birthplace: Montgomery County, TN
Mother: Mary Jackson
Birthplace: Rutherford County, TN
Physician: Dr. Jas. L. Morton

POTTS, ROBERT EARLE
Date of Funeral: Sep 19, 1927   10 a.m.
Casket: Oct White, size 3/6 &
Box, Hearse, Services $ 62.00
Date of Death: Sep 18, 1927, 10th District, Bedford County, TN
Place of Funeral: Cothran Yard
Interred: Cothran Yard
Date of Birth: Feb 29 (no date)
Age: 3y, 6m, 20d.
Color: White
Father: William Potts
Birthplace: Bedford County, TN
Mother: Addie Stem
Birthplace: Bedford County, TN
Physician: Dr. Culberson

PRICE, LORENZO DENTON
Date of Funeral: Nov 20, 2928   1 p.m.
Embalming $ 25.00
Casket: State Gray, Plush, ½ coach, size 6/3 &
Box, Hearse, Services   255.00
Burial Garment: Suit, Shirt, Collar, Tie   30.00
Hose   .50
Metal Box Covers   6.00
Grave Lining   3.00
Total: $ 319.00
Date of Death: Nov 18, 1928 at Home, 19th District, Bedford County, TN
Clergyman: Bro. Trotter

Interred: Willow Mount Cemetery, Shelbyville, TN
Date of Birth: Nov 6, 1859
Age: 612y, 1m, 12d.
Color: White – Occupation: Farmer
Married
Birthplace: Bedford County, TN
Father: Jas. Price
Birthplace: Bedford County, TN
Mother: Ann Johnson
Birthplace: Bedford County, TN
Physician: ____
Cause of Death: Suicide, Revolver wound of head.

PRICE, MRS. PEARL
Date of Funeral: May 27, 1929   10:30 a.m.
Casket: Oct Blk, E. Crape, size 5/9 &
Ambulance Trips $ 100.00
Date of Death: In Ambulance near House, 4th District, Bedford County, TN
Clergyman: Rufus Farrow
Interred: Hurricane Grove Cemetery
Date of Birth: Feb 20, 1929
Age: 44y, 3m, 6d.
Color: White – Occupation: At Home
Married
Birthplace: Bedford County, TN
Husband: Charles Price
Father: Russell Stubblefield
Birthplace: South Carolina
Mother: Martha Green
Birthplace: ____
Physician: Dr. W.A. Moon

PRINCE, (Infant of Mr. and Mrs. Clyde Prince)
Date of Funeral: Jul 6. 1926
Casket: Flat Top, L.S., size 2/0 & Box $ 12.50
Ordered by Bill Prince
Date of Death: Jul 5, 1926 at Shelbyville, TN
Interred: Houston Grave Yard
Date of Birth: July 5, 1926
Age: 0
Color: White
Birthplace: Shelbyville, TN
Father: Clyde Prince
Physician: Dr. Jas. L. Morton

PRINCE, MARION RHEA
Date of Funeral: May 19, 1927   11 a.m.
Casket: Oct White P.K., size 2/0 &
Box, Car, Services $ 35.00
Ordered by Ray Prince & G.M. Coop
Date of Death: May 18, 1927 at residence of G.M. Coop, 6th District of
Bedford County, TN
Place of Funeral: Cemetery, Bell Buckle, TN
Interred: Bell Buckle Cemetery
Date of Birth: Mar 2, 1927
Age: 1m, 25d.
Color: White
Birthplace: Nashville, TN
Last place of Residence, Nashville, TN
Father: Ray Prince
Birthplace: TN
Mother: Susie Bell Coop
Birthplace: Bedford County, TN
Physician: Dr. W.H. Avery

PRINCE, WILLIAM
Date of Funeral: Jul 15, 1927   10 a.m.
Casket: Steel Gray, E. Crape, size 6/3 &
Box, Hearse, Services $ 125.00
Burial Garment: Suit, Shirt, Collar, Tie   25.00
Metal Box Covers   6.00
Total: $ 156.00
Date of Death: Jul 14, 1927 at Home, Wartrace Pike
Place of Funeral: Home, Wartrace Pike
Clergyman: Dr. S.P. White & Rev. C. Lewis
Interred: Bedford (Cemetery)
Date of Birth: Mar 1, 1857
Age: 74y, 4m, 14d.
Color: White – Occupation: Farmer
Married
Birthplace: Bedford County, TN
Father: Jerry Prince
Birthplace: Cannon County, TN
Mother: Unknown
Physician: Dr. W.H. Avery

PROCTOR, MISS ELLA
Date of Funeral: Mar 6, 1926   2 p.m.
Removing Remains from County Farm to Pisgah $ 10.00
Casket: County Coffin B. size 5/9   12.00

Total: $ 22.00
Ordered by W.G. Rucker (Chairman)
Date of Death: Mar 5, 1926 at County Farm, Bedford County, TN
Place of Funeral: Pisgah Church Cemetery
Interred: Pisgah Grave Yard
Date of Birth: ____
Age: About 54 yrs.
Color: ____
Single
Birthplace: Bedford County, TN
Father: Jno. Proctor

PROSSER, GROVER HENRY
Date of Funeral: Jun 3, 1929   11 a.m.
Casket: Sq. Flat Top, Gray E. Crape, Size 6/3 &
Box, Hearse, Services $ 85.00
Ordered by T. Prosser
Date of Death: Home, T. Prosser, Shelbyville, TN
Clergyman: Elder Rufus Farrar
Interred: Hickory Hill Grave Yard (Chestnut Ridge)
Date of Birth: Nov 26, 1850
Age: 78y, 6m, 7d.
Color: White – Occupation: Drayman(?)
Widower
Birthplace: Bedford County, TN
Father: Grover Prosser
Birthplace: North Carolina
Mother: Polly Rose
Birthplace: North Carolina
Physician: Dr. Jas. L. Morton

PROSSER, HOYT
Date of Funeral: Nov 23, 1925   2 p.m.
Removing Remains $ 15.00
Metal Box Covers   5.00
Drayage   2.00
Total: $ 22.00
Ordered by Walace Prosser
Date of Death: Nov 21, 1925 at Nashville, TN
Place of Funeral: Shelbyville, TN
Clergyman: Dr. White
Interred: Holland Grave Yard
Date of Birth: ____
Age: 9 yrs.
Color: White

Cause of Death: Accident, hit by automobile

PUCKETT, MRS. MARTHA ANN
Date of Funeral: Mar 14, 1926   2:30 p.m.
Casket: Sil Gray, E. Crape, size 6/3 &
Box, Hearse, Services, Metal Covers $ 100.00
Burial Garment: Crape White Dress   20.00
Total: $ 120.00
Ordered by Willie Grooms
Date of Death: Mar 14, 1926 at Willie Grooms Home, Shelbyville, TN
Place of Funeral: Willie Grooms Home, Shelbyville, TN
Clergyman: Dr. S.P. White
Interred: Willow Mount Cemetery, Shelbyville,
Date of Birth: Apr 17, 1873
Age: 53 yrs
Widow
Birthplace: Bedford County, TN
Father: Henry F. Freeman
Birthplace: ____
Mother: Harriett Williams
Birthplace: ____
Physician: Dr. J.L. Morton

RANEY, MRS. WILLIE FLORENCE
Date of Funeral: Jan 15, 1926   1 p.m.
Casket: 509 Sil Gray Crape, size 5/4 &
Box, Hearse, Services $ 125.00
Metal Box Covers   5.00
Total: $ 130.00
Ordered by Robert Wright
Date of Death: Jan 14, 1926 at Hospital, Shelbyville, TN
Place of Funeral: Moores Chapel
Interred: Moores Chapel
Date of Birth: Oct 2, 1885
Age: 40 yrs.
Color: White – Occupation: Housewife
Married
Birthplace: Bedford County, TN
Husband: W.E. Raney
Father: Wm. N. Bradshaw
Birthplace: TN
Mother: Julia White
Birthplace: TN
Physician: Dr. J.T. Conditt

RANEY, ROBERT LEE
Date of Funeral: Sep 5, 1929   3 p.m.
Embalming $ 20.00
Casket: Oct Gray, plush, ½ couch, size 6/3   260.00
Box, Hearse, Services &
Burial Garment: Suit, Shirt, Collar, Tie   20.00
Underwear & Hose   xxx
Metal Box Covers   xxx
Total: $300.00
Ordered by Leonard Raney
Date of Death: Sep 4, 1929 at Home, 23rd District, Bedford County, TN
Clergyman: Rev. J.W. Cherry
Interred: Smiths Chapel Cemetery
Date of Birth: Jan 1, 1878
Age: 51y, 7m, 24d.
Married
Birthplace: Lincoln County, TN
Last place of Residence: Bedford County, TN
Father: Henry Raney
Birthplace: Lincoln County, TN
Mother: Molly Scott
Birthplace: Lincoln (County, TN)

Physician: Dr. T.J. Coble

RANSOM, WILLLIAM STREET
Date of Funeral: Aug 4, 1929   2:30 p.m.
Removing Remains, Dressing, etc &
Embalming $ 50.00
Casket: Gray State BC Nat., size 6/3   400.00
Metal Vault, Style, Clark   125.00
Total: $575.00
Ordered by W.S. Ransom
Date of Death: Aug 3, 1929 at Home, Nashville, TN
Place of Funeral: Willow Mount Cemetery, Shelbyville, TN
Clergyman: Rev. W.C. Creasman
Interred: Willow Mount Cemetery, Shelbyville, TN
Date of Birth: Feb 2, 1881
Age: 48y, 6m, 1d.
Color: White – Occupation: Lumber Manufacturer
Married
Birthplace: Rutherford County, TN
Last place of Residence: Nashville, TN
Father: Geo. W. Ransom
Birthplace: Rutherford County, TN
Mother: Margaret Buchanan
Birthplace: Davidson County, TN
Physician: Dr. Clinton Brush
Cause of Death: Suicide (Pistol Shot)

REAVIS, GEORGE ROBERT
Date of Funeral: Dec 20, 1927   2 p.m.
Shaving, Washing etc $ 5.00
Casket: Blk E. Crape, size 6/3 &
Box, Hearse, Services   100.00
Metal Box Covers   6.00
Black Bow Tie   .50
Grave Lining   3.00
Total: $114.50
Date of Death: Dec 20, 1927 at Home, Shelbyville, TN
Place of Funeral: Home, Shelbyville, TN
Clergyman: Bro. E.P. Watson
Interred: Willow Mount Cemetery, Shelbyville, TN
Date of Birth: Aug 1, 1856
Age: 71y, 4m, 19d.
Color: White – Occupation: Night Watchman
Married
Birthplace: Bedford County, TN

Father: David Reavis
Birthplace: Bedford County, TN
Mother: Elizabeth Hurdlow
Birthplace: Bedford County, TN
Physician: Dr. W.H. Avery

REED, JAMES GUY
Date of Funeral: Apr 9, 1929   3:30 p.m.
Casket: Oct Gray, Crape, size 6/3 &
Box, Metal Covers, Robe, Hose, Hearse, Hose $ 110.00
Date of Death: Apr 9, 1929 at Home, 6th District, Bedford County, TN
Place of Funeral: Harts Chapel
Interred: Harts Chapel Cemetery
Date of Birth: Nov 2, 1881
Age: 47y, 5m, 7d.
Color: White – Occupation: Farmer
Married
Birthplace: Bedford County, TN
Father: Pete Reed
Birthplace: ____
Mother: Mandy Biggers
Birthplace: ____
Physician: Dr. W.H. Avery

REED, LIFUS OLLIE
Date of Funeral: Apr 30, 1928   3 p.m.
Casket: Oct Gray, plush, size 63 &
Box, Hearse, Services $ 200.00
Metal Box Covers   6.00
Total: $ 206.00
Ordered by Sons
Date of Death: Apr 19, 1928 at Home, 25th District, Bedford County, TN
Place of Funeral: Smiths Chapel
Clergyman: Rev. J.W. Cherry
Interred: Smiths Chapel Cemetery
Date of Birth: Nov 30, 1866
Age: 61y, 4m, 19d.
Color: White – Occupation: Farmer
Married
Birthplace: Bedford County, TN
Father: Ben Reed
Birthplace: Bedford County, TN
Mother: Jane Snell
Birthplace: Bedford County, TN

REED, MARGARET ELLA MAY
Date of Funeral: Nov 8, 1927   1 p.m.
Casket: Flat Top L.S., size 2/0 & Box $ 15.00
Date of Death: Nov 7, 1927 at Home, Shelbyville, TN
Interred: Christiana, TN
Date of Birth: Feb 3, 1927
Age: 9m, 4d.
Birthplace: Bedford County, TN
Father: Jim Reed
Birthplace: Rutherford County, TN
Mother: Maggie Smith
Birthplace: Murry (Maury) County, TN
Physician: Dr. J.E. Bias

REED, MRS. JANE
Date of Funeral: Apr 10, 1925   2 p.m.
Casket: Gray E. Crape, size 5/9 &
Box, Services $ 110.00
Date of Death: Apr 9, 1925 at 23rd District, Bedford County, TN
Placĕ of Funeral: New Hope
Clergyman: Dr. White
Interred: New Hope Cemetery
Date of Birth: Feb 4, 1842
Age: 83y, 2m, 5d.
Color: White
Birthplace: Bedford County, TN
Physician: Dr. Fuston

REESE, (Infant Son of Mr. and Mrs. Willie G. Reese)
Date of Funeral: Aug 13, 1929   2 p.m.
Casket: Flat Top L.S., size 2/0 $ 15.00
Date of Death: Aug 12, 1929 at Home, 8th District, Moore County, TN
Place of Funeral: Home, 8th District, Moore County, TN
Interred: Mt. Herman Cemetery
Date of Birth: Aug 12, 1929
Age: Still Born
Color: White
Birthplace: Moore County, TN
Father: Willie G. Reese
Birthplace: Moore County, TN
Mother: Lizzie Petty
Birthplace: Bedford County, TN
Physician: Dr. J.T. Conditt

REID, FRANCIS ELOISE
Date of Funeral: Feb 5, 1929   10 a.m.
Casket: Flat Top L.S., size 3/6 &
Box, Metals (Ambulance) $ 33.00
Date of Death: Feb 4, 1929 at Bedford County Hospital
Place of Funeral: Home, Shelbyville, TN
Interred: Shelbyville Mills
Date of Birth: Mar 17, 1925
Age: 2y, 10m, 18d.
Color: White
Birthplace: Bedford County, TN
Father: William Reid
Birthplace: Huntsville, Alabama
Mother: Ethel Clanton
Birthplace: Bedford County, TN
Physician: Dr. Jas. L. Morton

REYNOLDS, THOMAS BENTON
Date of Funeral: Jan 24, 2929   2 p.m.
Casket: Oct Blk E. Crape, size 6/3 &
Box, Hearse, Robe, Metals, Services: $95.00
Date of Death: Jan 24, 1929 at Bedford County, Hospital, Shelbyville, TN
Place of Funeral: Home, W.W. Sanders
Clergyman: Dr. Julian Sibley
Interred: Willow Mount Cemetery, Shelbyville, TN
Date of Birth: Sep 29, 1894
Age: 34y, 3m, 25d.
Color: White – Occupation: Farmer
Married
Birthplace: Marshall County, TN
Last place of Residence: Bedford County, TN
Father: Anzior(?) Reynolds
Birthplace: Moore County, TN
Mother: Clarisa Reavis
Birthplace: Lincoln County, TN

ROBERTSON, MRS. MATTIE BELL LENTZ
Date of Funeral: Dec 5, 1929   1 p.m.
Casket: White plush, ½ couch, size 6/3 &
Box, Hearse, Services $ 260.00
Metal Box Covers   6.00
Total: $ 266.00
Date of Death: Dec 4, 1929 at Bedford County Hospital, Shelbyville, TN
Place of Funeral: Crowells Chapel
Clergyman: Rev. Kelly

Interred: Crowells Chapel Cemetery
Date of Birth: Nov 1, 1897
Age: 32y, 1m, 3d.
Color: White – Occupation: At Home
Married
Birthplace: Bedford County, TN
Husband: J.D. Robertson
Father: John H. Lentz
Birthplace: Bedford County, TN
Mother: Tennie Crowell
Birthplace: Bedford County, TN
Physician: Dr. W.H. Avery

ALLIE MARSH ROBINSON
Date of Funeral: Feb 8, 1925   2 p.m.
Casket: Gray Eng. Crape, size 6/3 &
Embalming, Metal Box Covers, Robe, Services $125.00
Date of Death: Feb 7, 1925 at Bedford County Hospital
Place of Funeral: Flat Creek
Clergyman: Bro. Watson
Interred: Flat Creek Cemetery
Date of Birth: Sep 2, 1881
Age: 43 yrs.
Color: White – Occupation: Farmer
Birthplace: Bedford County, TN
Physician: J.T. Conditt
Cause of Death: Pneumonia

ROBINSON, EVA ELIZABETH
Date of Funeral: Mar 1, 1925
Casket: White, size 2/0 & Box $ 10.00
Date of Death: Feb 28, 1925 at 8th District, Bedford County, TN
Interred: Burns Cemetery

ROBINSON, JAMES MALCOM
Date of Funeral: Jan 25, 1929   3 p.m.
Casket: Oct, White plush, size 2/6 &
Clark Vault, Hearse, Service $ 90.00
Date of Death: Jan 23, 1929 at 8th District, Bedford County, TN
Place of Funeral: Home, 8th District, Bedford County, TN
Clergyman: ____ Pack
Date of Birth: Sep 8, 1928
Age: 15 days
Color: White
Birthplace: Bedford County, TN

Father: J.M. Robinson
Birthplace: Bedford County, TN
Mother: Mattie Beavers
Birthplace: Bedford County, TN
Physician: Dr. Jas. L. Morton

ROBINSON, MRS. NETTIE ALMA
Date of Funeral: Jul 6, 1925   2.p.m.
Embalming $ 20.00
Casket: Sil Gray, Crape. Size 6/3 &
Hearse, Service   125.00
Metal Box Covers   5.00
Total: $150.00
Date of Death: Jul 5, 1925 at 22nd District, Bedford County, TN
Place of Funeral: New Herman
Interred: Flat Creek Cemetery
Date of Birth: Sep 7, 1883
Age: 42 yrs.
Color: White
Widow
Birthplace: Bedford County, TN
Husband: Ollie Robinson
Father: James Gilliland
Birthplace: Alabama
Mother: Kate Mullins
Birthplace: TN
Physician: Dr. Conditt

ROGERS, MRS. FANNIE LOUISE
Date of Funeral: Feb 11, 1928   1 p.m.
Casket: Oct Gray, size 6/3 &
Box, Hearse, Services $ 200.00
Burial Garment: Silk Dress   31.50
Slippers   4.50
Metal Box Covers   6.00
Truck, Car, & Driver   3.00
Total: $ 245.00
Date of Death: Feb 10, 1928 at Home, 23rd District, Bedford County, TN
Place of Funeral: New Hope Church
Clergyman: Rev. S.A. Jones
Interred: New Hope Cemetery
Date of Birth: Mar 12, 1863
Age: 64y, 10m, 29d.
Married
Birthplace: Bedford County, TN

Husband: J. Brownlow Rogers
Father: Lytle Hickerson
Birthplace: Coffee County, TN
Mother: Nannie Moore
Birthplace: Bedford County, TN
Physician: Dr. T.J. Coble

ROSBOROUGH, MADISON CLAY
Date of Funeral: May 14, 1927   12 n.
Casket: Oct Blk, B.C., size 6/3 &
Box, Hearse, Services $190.00
Burial Garment: Suit, Collar, Shirt, Tie   28.00
Metal Box Covers   6.00
Total: $224.00
Date of Death: May 13, 1927 at Home, 5th District, Bedford County, TN
Place of Funeral: Unity
Clergyman: _____ Brown
Interred: Unity Cemetery
Date of Birth: Jul 31, 1860
Age: 67y, 9m, 13d.
Birthplace: Bedford County, TN
Father: John Rosborough
Birthplace: Lincoln County, TN
Mother: Sarah Smith
Birthplace: Lincoln County, TN
Physician: Dr. A.E. Fuston

RUCKER, MRS. MALISIA ANN
Date of Funeral: Nov 5, 1927   2 p.m.
Casket: 536 Gray, plush, size 6/3 &
Box, Hearse, Service $ 200.00
Metal Box Covers   6.00
Grave Lining   6.00
Total: $ 212.00
Date of Death: Nov 4, 1927 at Home, Shelbyville, TN
Place of Funeral: Home, Shelbyville, TN
Clergyman: rev. J.W. Cherry
Interred: Willow Mount Cemetery, Shelbyville, TN
Date of Birth: Apr 8, 1850
Age: 77y, 6m, 27d.
Color: White – Occupation: Housewife
Married
Birthplace: Bedford County, TN
Husband: Wm. G. Rucker
Father: Henry Jones

Birthplace: TN
Mother: Nancy Lyle
Birthplace: North Carolina
Physician: Dr. T.R. Ray

RUSS, LEE H.
Date of Funeral: May 14, 1925   11:30 a.m.
Removing Remains to Cemetery $12.00
Metal Box Covers   5.00
Grave Lining   1.50
Drayage   1.50
Total: $20.50
Date of Death: May 13, 1825 at Montgomery, Alabama
Place of Funeral: Shelbyville, TN
Clergyman: Dr. Robinson
Interred: Willow Mount Cemetery, Shelbyville, TN
Date of Birth: _____
Age: 78 yrs.
Color: White
No other information

SAINES, CHARLES CASPER
Date of Funeral: Dec 26, 1929   2 p.m.
Casket: Sq. Flat Top. Size 6/3 &
Box, Hearse, Service $ 62.00
Date of Death: Dec 25, 1929 at Home, Shelbyville Mills
Place of Funeral: Bethney (Coffee County, TN)
Clergyman: Rev. J.E. Trotter
Interred: Bethney Cemetery
Date of Birth: Jan 19, 1881
Age: 48y, 11m, 6d.
Color: White – Occupation: Farmer
Married
Birthplace: Coffee County, TN
Last place of Residence: Bedford County, TN
Father: A.J. Saines
Birthplace: Coffee County, TN
Mother: Rebecca Carroll
Birthplace: Coffee County, TN
Physician: Dr. W.H. Avery

SAINES, MRS. REBECCA
Date of Funeral: Dec 31, 1928   1.p.m.
Casket: Blk Oct Crape, size 5/3 &
Box, Hearse, Service $ 125.00
Burial Garment: Black Silk Dress   30.00
Metal Box Covers   6.00
Total: $ 161.00
Date of Death: Dec 30, 1928 at Home of Thos. Saines at the Mills
Place of Funeral; Blanton Grave Yard, Coffee County, TN
Interred: Blanton Grave Yard
Date of Birth: ____
Age: 66y, 3m, 23d.
Widow
Birthplace: Coffee County, TN
Father: Sam Carroll
Birth place: TN
Mother: Unknown
Physician: Dr. W.H. Avery

SANDERS, JAMES ANDERSON
Date of Funeral: Mar 30, 1928   11 a.m.
Embalming $ 20.00
Casket: Oct Blk. Size 6/3 &
Hearse, Services, Box   175.00
Burial Garment: Suit, Collar, Shirt, Tie, Sox   20.00

Metal Box Covers   6.00
Grave Lining   3.00
Total: $224.00
Date of Death: Mar 28, 1928 at 7th District, Bedford County, TN
Place of Funeral: Home, Bedford County, TN
Clergyman: Rev. J.W. Cherry
Interred: Willow Mount Cemetery, Shelbyville, TN
Date of Birth: Mar 25, 1842
Age: 86 yrs.
Color: White – Occupation: Farmer
Married
Birthplace: Moore County, TN
Last place of Residence: Bedford County, TN
Father: Wm. B. Sanders
Birthplace: Franklin County, TN
Mother: Palsie Driver
Birthplace: Lincoln County, TN
Physician: Dr. T.R. Ray

SAVAGE, JAMES WILLIAM
Date of Funeral: Feb 25, 1929   2 p.m.
Casket: Oct H.Y., plush, size 3/0 &
Box, Hearse, Service, Metals, Grave Lining $ 65.00
Date of Death: Feb 23, 1929 at Home, Shelbyville, TN
Place of Funeral: Home Shelbyville, TN
Interred: Willow Mount Cemetery, Shelbyville, TN
Date of Birth: Nov 11, 1928
Age: 3m, 12d.
Birthplace: Bedford County, TN
Father: Archie Savage
Birthplace: Bedford County, TN
Mother: Gladys Reed
Birthplace: Lewis County, TN
Physician: Dr. W. Avery

SAVAGE, SUSIE LOU
Date of Funeral: Jul 8, 1926   10 a.m.
Casket: White, plush, size 6/3 &
Box Metals, Hearse, Embalming, Dress, Services $ 300.00
Date of Death: Jul 6, 9126 at Hospital, Shelbyville, TN
Place of Funeral: Home, Shelbyville, TN
Clergyman: Rev. S.A. Jones
Interred: Jul 8, 1926
Date of Birth: Dec 15, 1910
Age: 16 yrs

Color: White – Occupation: School Girl
Single
Birthplace: Bedford County, TN
Father: Myrtle Savage
Mother: Josephine Nowlin

SANDERS, MRS. J.H.   (Out of Line)
Date of Funeral: Mar 26, 1927   10 a.m.
Casket: Sil Gray, E. Crape, size 6/3 &
Box, Hearse, Services $ 139.00
Burial Garment: White Silk Dress   30.00
Metal Box Covers   6.00
Total: $ 166.00
Ordered by J.H. Sanders
Date of Death: Mar 25, 1927 at Home, Shelbyville, TN
Place of Funeral: North Fork Church
Interred: Pressgrove Grave Yard
Date of Birth: Mar 28, 1859
Age: 67y, 11m, 25d.
Color: White – Occupation: Housewife
Married
Birthplace: Bedford County, TN
Husband: J.H. Sanders
Father: Geo. Brown
Birthplace: South Carolina
Mother: Lucy Park(er?) or Parks
Birthplace: Don't Know
Physician: Not Any
Cause of Death: Found dead in bed.

SCALES, MRS. MOLLIE C.
Date of Funeral: Nov 24, 1924   2 p.m.
Embalming $ 20.00
Casket: Nat. Gray, B.C. State, Full Hinge Top   400.00
Metal Vault, Style, Clark   125.00
Drayage on 6 chairs   4.00
Grave Lining   1.50
To cover dirt   1.00
Total: $551.00
Ordered by Joe P. Scales
Date of Death: Nov 23, 1924 at Bedford County, TN
Place of Funeral: Home
Clergyman: W.J. Collier
Interred: Willow Mount Cemetery, Shelbyville, TN
Date of Birth: Nov 12, 1855

Age: 69 yrs.
Married
Birthplace: Bedford County, TN
Husband: Joe P. Scales
Father: J.A. Cunningham
Mother: Elizabeth Gregg
Physician: Dr. G.W. Moody
Cause of Death: Heart Failure

SCOTT, AFFIE McLANE (Col)
Date of Funeral: Dec 19, 1928   11:30 a.m.
Casket: Oct Gray, E. Crape, size 6/3 B &
Hearse to Nashville, Metals, Services $ 142.00
Date of Death: Dec 16, 1928 at Vanderbilt Hospital, Nashville, TN
Place of funeral: Mt. Zion, Bedford County, TN
Interred: Mt. Zion
Date of Birth: Dec 17, 1903
Age: 25y, 2d.
Color: Colored, Occupation: House wife
Married
Birthplace: Bedford County, TN
Last place of Residence: Nashville, TN
Father: Abraham McLane
Birthplace: Lincoln County, TN
Mother: Laura Ditto
Birthplace: Bedford County, TN

SHARP, MRS. PALESTINE
Date of Funeral: at Houston, Texas
Removing Remains from Train to Cemetery and Service $15.00
Metal Box Covers   5.00
Drayage on Box   1.00
Grave Lining   2.00
Total: $23.00
No other information

SHEARIN, MRS. ANNIE
Date of Funeral: Sep 15, 1929   2 p.m.
Embalming $ 20.00
Casket: Oct Gray, plush, size 6/0 &
Hearse, Services, Drayage, etc   175.00
Metal Vault, Style, Clark   125.00
Total: 320.00
Ordered by Children
Date of Death: Sep 14, 1929 at D.E. Crowell, 11th District, Bedford Co., TN

Place of Funeral: Home, D.E. Crowell, 11th District of Bedford County, TN
Clergyman: Rev. Chas. Armstrong
Interred: Crowell Grave Yard
Date of Birth: Oct 31, 1861
Age: 67y, 10m, 14d.
Color: White – Occupation: At Home
Birthplace: Bedford County, TN
Father: Strick Parsons
Birthplace: TN
Mother: Jennie Crowell
Birthplace: TN
Physician: Dr. Ben L. Burdett

SHEARIN, WM. MATTHEW
Date of Funeral: Apr 21, 1927   3 p.m.
Casket: Blk B.C., State, size 6/3 &
Hearse, Services $ 300.00
Metal Vault, Style, Clark   125.00
Burial Garment: Underwear, Sox   2.25
Grave Lining   3.00
Total: $ 450.25
Ordered by Mrs. Ida Shearin
Date of Death: Apr 20, 1927 at Home, Shelbyville, TN
Place of Funeral: Home, Shelbyville, TN
Interred: Willow Mount Cemetery, Shelbyville, TN
Date of Birth: Sep 24, 1860
Age: 66y, 6m, 26d.
Color: White – Occupation: Farmer
Married
Birthplace: Bedford County, TN
Father: Mathew Shearin
Birthplace: Bedford County, TN
Mother: Elizabeth Gant
Birthplace: Bedford County, TN
Physician: Dr. Ben L. Burdett

SHERRILL, PAUL A.
Date of Funeral: Oct 9, 1928   2 p.m.
Removing Remains, 2 house trips and Services $ 35.00
Metal Box Covers   6.00
Grave Lining   6.00
Services   5.00
Total: $ 46.00
Date of Death: Oct 8, 1928 at Bruceton, TN
Place of Funeral: Near Normandy, TN

Clergyman: Rev. Robertson & Rev. Trotter
Interred: Green Grave Yard
Date of Birth: Apr 8 (no year given)
Age: 27y, 5m, 22d.
Color: White – Occupation: Rail Road Brakeman
Married
Cause of Death: Rail Road Accident

SHOFFNER, MR. JOHN E.

Date of Funeral: Mar 29, 1925 2 p.m.	
Embalming	$ 15.00
Casket: State Gray B.C., size 6/3	325.00
Cedar Box	25.00
Metal Box Covers	5.00
Total:	$ 370.00

Ordered by C.L. Shoffner
Date of Death: Mar 27, 1925 at Shelbyville, TN
Place of Funeral: Jenkins Chapel
Clergyman: Dr. Robinson
Interred: Jenkins Chapel Cemetery
Date of Birth: Jan 15, 1847
Age: 78y, 2m, 12d.
Color: White – Occupation: Farmer Banker
Married
Birthplace: Bedford County, TN
Physician: Dr. Fuston

SHOFFNER, MRS. MARY E.

Date of Funeral: Mar 25, 1926 2 p.m.	
Embalming	$ 15.00
Casket: Chatt State size 6/3 &	
Hearse, Services	325.00
Outside Case: Cedar	25.00
Burial Garment: Silk Dress	38.00
Slippers	3.00
Metal Box Covers	5.00
Drayage, Extra Chairs	4.00
Total:	$ 415.00

Date of Death: Mar 23, 1926 at Home, Shelbyville, TN
Place of Burial: Jenkins Chapel Cemetery
Clergyman: Dr. Armstrong
Date of Birth: Sep 30, 1850
Age: 75 yrs.
Color: White
Widow

Birthplace: Bedford County, TN
Husband: Jno. E. Shoffner
Father: Wm. H. Young
Mother: Katherine Hooser
Physician: Dr. A.E. Fuston

SHOFNER, EDGAR
Date of Funeral: Dec 28, 1929   2 p.m.
Removing Remains from Bell Buckle to Shelbyville then to Flat Creek &
Hearse, Services $ 25.00
Metal Box Covers   6.00
Grave Lining, Drayage, etc.   7.50
Total: $ 38.50
Date of Death: Dec 25, 1929 at Toledo, Ohio
Place of Funeral: Flat Creek, TN
Clergyman: Rev. Geo. Gowan
Interred: Flat Creek Cemetery
Date of Birth: ____
Widower
Last place of Residence: Toledo, Ohio

SHOFNER, JOHN CLAY
Date of Funeral: (Nashville, TN) Shelbyville, TN 11:30 a.m. &
Sep 17, 1925
Removing Remains from Depot to Cemetery $ 15.00
Casket: Sil Oct H.. Orval Tap &
Metal Box Covers   5.00
Dirt Covering   1.50
Grave Lining   2.00
Drayage, Box, Chairs, etc   1.50
Total: $ 25.00
Date of Death: Sep 15, 1925   11:30 a.m.
Place of Death: Nashville, TN
Place of Funeral: Nashville & Shelbyville, TN
Clergyman: Dr. J.N. Cherry at Selbyville, TN
Interred: Willow Mount Cemetery
Date of Birth: _____
Age: 72 yrs
Color: White
Married
Cause of Death: Uremia

SHOFNER, MARY LEONA
Date of Funeral: Sep 23, 1925   3 p.m.
Embalming $ 20.00

Casket: Sil Gray, plush, size 6/3 & Box	$ 200.00
Box, Metal Box Covers	5.00
Total:	$ 225.00

Ordered by Geo. Shofner
Date of Death: Sep 22, 1925 at 24th District, Bedford County, TN
Interred: Flat Creek Cemetery
Date of Birth: Jan 20, 2859
Age: 66 yrs
Color: White – Occupation: Housewife
Married
Birthplace: TN
Husband: Geo. Shofner
Physician: Dr. Conditt
Cause of Death: Cancer

SHRIVER, JACK
Date of Funeral: Dec 3, 1924   1 p.m.

Removing Remains from Train	$ 12.50
Drayage	1.00
Metal Covers	5.00
Grave Lining	1.50
Dirt Cover	1.00
Total:	$ 21.00

Ordered by Chas. Taylor
No other information

SHUMARD, MISS LIZZIE FRANK
Date of Funeral: Nov 18, 1927   1 p.m.

Embalming	$ 20.00
Casket: State Metal, size 6/3	650.00
Metal Vault, Style, Clark	125.00
Slippers	5.00
Hearse Trip to Tullahoma	25.00
Telephone	2.00
R.R. Fare & Express Baggage on Ambulance	6.00
Remains to St. Louis, Mo.	18.25
Total:	$851.28

Date of Death: Nov 17, 1927 at Hotel Dixie, Shelbyville, TN
Place of Funeral: Presbyterian Church
Clergyman: Dr. J.W. Cherry & Dr. Sibley
Interred: St. Louis, MO.
Date of Birth: Unknown
Age: 70 yrs.
Color: White - Single

Birthplace: Unknown
Last place of residence: Shelbyville, TH
Father: Dr. Ben Shumard
Birthplace: Unknown
Mother: Elizabeth Allen
Birthplace: Unknown
Physician: Dr. G.W. Moody
Cause of Death: Colitis

SIMS, JAMES AUSTIN
Date of Funeral: Nov 12, 1926   2 p.m.
Casket: State White, plush, size 4/10 &
Not Hinge Top $ 150.00
Metal Vault, Style, Clark   125.00
Total: $ 250.00
Ordered by W.A. Sims
Date of Death: Nov 11, 1926 at Home, Shelbyville, TN
Place of Funeral: Home, Shelbyville, TN
Clergyman: Dr. J.W. Cherry
Interred: Willow Mount Cemetery, Shelbyville, TN
Date of Birth: Nov 25, 1922
Age: 4 yrs.
Color: White
Birthplace: Murfreesboro, TN
Last place of Residence, Shelbyville, TN
Father: W.A. Sims
Birthplace: Nashville, TN
Mother: Allie E. Sims
Birthplace: Nashville, TN
Physician: Dr. W.H. Avery

SIPSEY, MRS. MOLLIE
Date of Funeral: Jan 12, 1926   2 p.m.
Casket: Chatt. B.A., size 6/0 &
Box, Hearse, Services, Robe $ 50.00
Ordered by W.H Sipsey
Date of Death: Jan 11, 1926 at Home, Sylvan Cotton Mills
Place of Funeral: Home, Sylvan Cotton Mills
Clergyman: Dr. Watson
Interred: Near Sylvan Cotton Mills
Date of Birth: 1867
Age: 59 yrs.
Color: White – Occupation: Housewife
Married
Husband: W.H. Sipsey

Physician: Dr. W.H. Avery

SMITH, ARTHUR EARNEST
Date of Funeral: Oct 14, 1929   3 p.m.
Removing Remains to Shelbyville from Central Hospital $ 15.00
Embalming   20.00
Casket: Oct Gray, plush, ½ couch, size 6/3 &
Box, Hearse, Services   265.00
Burial Garment: Suit, Shirt, Collar, Tie   30.00
Metal Box Covers   6.00
Grave Lining & etc   10.00
Flowers   30.00
Closed Cars   8.00
Total: 384.00
Ordered by Mrs. A(?). E. Smith, 1123 Brook St., Louisville, KY, and
Mattie Brinkley. 6165 Winthorp Ave., Chicago, ILL
Date of Death: Oct 13, 1929
At Central Hospital, Nashville, TN
Interred: Richmond, TN
Date of Birth: May 25, 1878
Age: 51y, 4m, 18d.
Color: White – Occupation: Farmer
Married
Birthplace: Bedford County, TN
Last place of Residence: Central Hospital, Nashville, TN
Father: Thomas Hunter Smith
Birthplace: Bedford County, TN
Mother: Betty Williams
Birthplace: Bedford County, TN

SMITH, BESSIE
Date of Funeral: Apr 21, 1927   12 N
Removing remains from Train $ 15.00
Telephone   4.67
Express   37.24
Coach to Chicago – Fred A. Johnson, Med.   115.00
Total: 175.91
No other information

SMITH, GEORGE C.
Date of Funeral: Aug 15, 1926   1 a.m.
Embalming   20.00
Casket: Solid Walnut state, size 6/3 &
Burial Garment: Gray Suit   28.00
Underwear, Sox   2.00

Total: $ 300.00
Ordered by Mrs. Della Smith
Date of Death: Aug 14, 1926
Place of Death: Home, 22nd District, Bedford County, TN
Place of Funeral: Center Church
Interred: Center Church Cemetery
Date of Birth: May 12, 1857
Age: 69 yrs.
Color: White – Occupation: Farmer
Married
Birthplace: Bedford County, TN
Father: Jarrell B. Smith
Birthplace: TN
Mother: Sophia Ann Gammill
Birthplace: TN
Physician: De. Conditt

SMITH, MRS GEORGIA ANN BEARDEN
Date of Funeral: Jul 15, 1928   2 p.m.
Casket: Oct Gray, E. Crape, size 5/9 &
Box, Hearse, Services, Metals, Grave Lining $ 90.00
Ordered by F.R. Bearden
Date of Death: Jul 13. 1928 at Home of F.R. Bearden, Shelbyville, TN
Place of Funeral: Home of F.R. Bearden, Shelbyville, TN
Clergyman: Rev. Frank Tinder
Interred: willow Mount Cemetery, Shelbyville, TN
Date of Birth: Apr 9, 1867
Age: 71y, 3m, 4d.
Color: White – Occupation: Housewife
Widow
Father: Ely Bearden
Birthplace: TN
Mother: Winnie Stephens
Birthplace: Bedford County, TN
Physician: Not Any
Cause of Death: Found dead in bed.

SMITH, MRS. GEORGIA ROSE
Date of Funeral: Dec 22, 1929   3 p.m.
Casket: Oct Gray, size 6/3 &
Box, Hearse, Metals, Lining, Services $ 125.00
Date of Death: Dec 21, 1929 at Home, Shelbyville, TN
Place of Funeral: Cres. Church, Shelbyville, TN
Clergyman: Dr. J.S. Sibley
Interred: Willow Mount Cemetery, Shelbyville, TN

Date of Birth: Jul 28, 1851
Age: 78y, 4m, 23d.
Color: White – Occupation: At Home
Widow
Birthplace: Columbus, Miss.
Last place of Residence: Shelbyville, TN
Husband: B.F. Smith (deceased)
Father: ____ Baty
Birthplace: Virginia
Mother: Sarah Stocton(?)
Birthplace: North Carolina
Physician: Dr. T.J. Coble

SMITH, PAUL R.
Date of Funeral: Dec 28, 1929   11 a.m.
Removing Remains from Bell Buckle to Paul Smith to Bedford $30.00
Hearse, Services, Metal Boards   6.00
Grave Lining, Drayage, Truck   6.00
Total: $42.00
Date of Death: Dec 25, 1929 at Toledo, Ohio
Place of Funeral: Bedford County, TN
Clergyman: Rev. R.L. Stem
Interred: Bedford, TN
Date of Birth: Mar 13, 1894
Age: 35y, 9m, 15d.
Color: White
No other information

SNELL, LUCIEL JOSEPHINE
Date of Funeral: Jul 7, 1926
Casket: Oct White P.K., size 2/6 &
Box, Car, Services $ 23.00
Ordered by Thompson Snell
Date of Death: Jul 6, 1926 at Bedford County, TN
Place of Funeral: Willow Mount Cemetery, Shelbyville, TN
Clergyman: Dr. J.W. Cherry
Interred: Willow Mount Cemetery, Shelbyville, TN
Date of Birth: Sep 17, 1925
Age: 9m.
Color: White
Birthplace: Bedford County, TN
Father: Thompson Snell
Mother: Lena May Johns
Physician: Dr. T.R. Ray

SNELL, MRS. MAGGIE ANGELINE
Date of Funeral: Sep 9, 1928   2:30 p.m.
Embalming $ 20.00
Casket: Oct Sil Gray, E. Crape, size 6/3 &
Box, Hearse, Services   125.00
Metal Box Covers   6.00
Total: $151.00
Ordered by Estate
Date of Death: Sep 9, 1929 at Home of Mrs. Bridges of Bedford County, TN
Place of Funeral: M.E. Church, Singleton, TN
Clergyman: Rev. J.W. Cherry
Interred: Pisgah
Date of Birth: Nov 25, 1858
Age: 69y, 9m, 14d.
Color: White – Occupation: Housewife
Widow
Father: Asa Elkins
Birthplace: ____
Mother: Angeline Huffman
Birthplace: Bedford County, TN
Physician: Dr. Sutton

SNELL, VERNA A.
Date of Funeral: Jul 28, 1929   3 p.m.
Casket: Oct Gray L.S., size 6/3 &
Box, Hearse, Services $ 135.00
Metal Box Covers   6.00
Total: $ 141.00
Date of Death: Jul 27, 1929 at Home, 24th District, Bedford County, TN
Clergyman: Rev. Geo. Gowan
Interred: Flay Creek Cemetery
Date of Birth: Oct 24, 1889
Age: 39y, 9m, 3d.
Married
Birthplace: Bedford County, TN
Father: James G. Snell
Birthplace: Bedford County, TN
Mother: Fannie Rainey
Birthplace: Bedford County, TN
Physician: Dr. J.T. Conditt

SNODDY, MRS. ANNA C.
Date of Funeral: Dec 17, 1924   2:30 p.m.
Embalming $ 15.00
Casket: Gray B.C., size 6/3   185.00

Metal Vault, Style, Clark $ 125.00
Total: $325 .00
Date of Death: Dec 16, 1924 at Shelbyville, TN
Place of Funeral: Shelbyville, TN
Clergyman: Dr. C. Hinkle
Date of Burial: Dec 17, 1924
Interred: Willow Mount Cemetery, Shelbyville, TH
No other information

SORREL, J.E.
Date of Funeral: Jan 2, 1929   2 p.m.
Casket: Flat Top, size 4/6 $15.00
Date of Death: Jan 1, 1929 at 22nd District, Bedford County, TN
Place of Funeral: Hurricane Grave Yard
Interred: Hurricane Grave Yard
Date of Birth: Oct 3, 1923
Age: 5y, 2m, 29d.
Color: White
Birthplace: Bedford County, TN
Father: Logan Sorrel
Birthplace: Bedford County, TN
Mother: Lora Pierce
Birthplace: Bedford County, TN
Physician: Dr. ____

SPRINGFIELD, ED
Date of Funeral: Feb 12, 1928
Casket: B. Pauper, size 6/3 $ 12.00
Ordered by County Judge C.C. Phillips
Date of Death: Feb 10, 1928 at 25th District, Bedford County, TN
Interred: Roberts Grave Yard
Date of Birth: Unknown
Age: About 45
Color: White – Occupation: Painter
Married
Birthplace: Chattanooga, TN
Physician: Not Any
Cause of Death: Found dead in his room.

STEPHENS, MRS. ELLEN
Date of Funeral: Nov 7, 1927   12 n
Embalming $ 20.00
Casket: Oct Blk, E. Crape, size 6/3 &
Box, Hearse, Services   100.00
Burial Garment: Gray Silk Dress   20.00

Silk Hose	$ 1.50
Metal Box Covers	6.00
Total:	$147.50

Ordered by Geo. Stephens
Date of Death: Nov 6, 1927 at Home of Geo. Stephens,
22nd District of Bedford Co9unty, TN
Place of Funeral: County Line
Interred: County Line Cemetery
Date of Birth: Mar 20, 1864
Age: 63y, 7m, 15d.
Color: White – Occupation: Housewife
Widow
Birthplace: Bedford County, TN
Father: John Sons
Birthplace: TN
Mother: Nellie Bishop
Birthplace: TN
Physician: J.L. Conditt

STOKES, ED COOPER
Date of Funeral: Dec 19, 1929   1 p.m.

Embalming	$ 20.00
Casket: 1010. State Gray, size 6/3x &	
Box, Hearse, Service, Grave Lining, Drayage, etc	325.00
Metal Box Covers	5.00
Total:	$ 350.00

Ordered by Prewit Stokes
Date of Death: Dec 18, 1929 at Bedford County Hospital, Shelbyville, TN
Place of Funeral: Home, Rail Road
Clergyman: Rev. Mayberry
Interred: Willow Mount Cemetery, Shelbyville, TN
Date of Birth: Sep 13, 1876
Age: 53y, 3m, 5d.
Color: White – Occupation: Brakeman
Widower
Birthplace: Bedford County, TN
Father: Jas. (Jos.?) A. Stokes
Birthplace: Bedford County, TN
Mother: Cleo(?) Christian
Birthplace: Bedford County,
Physician: Dr. T.J. Coble

STUBBLEFIELD, S. RUSSELL
Date of Funeral: Apr 18, 1929

Casket: County B., size 6/3	$ 12.00

Hearse $ 10.00
Total: $22.00
Date of Death: Apr 17, 1929   10:30 a.m.
Place of Death: Home, 4th District, Bedford County, TN
Place of Funeral: Bell Buckle Cemetery
Interred: Bell Buckle, TN
Date of Birth: Apr 18, 1858
Age: 70 yrs.
Color: White – Occupation: Merchant
Married
Birthplace: Georgia
Last place of Residence: TN
Father: Unknown
Mother: Unknown
Physician: Dr. W.A. Moon, Bell Buckle

SULLIVAN, EDWIN
Date of Funeral: Aug 30, 1927
Casket: Flat Top. Size 4/6 &
Hearse, Services, Box, Clothes $ 55.00
Ordered by C.T. Sullivan
Date of Death: Aug 29, 1927 at Bedford County Hospital, Shelbyville, TN
Place of Funeral: Burns
Clergyman: Rev. Henley
Interred: Burns Cemetery
Date of Birth: Feb 11, 1919
Age: 8y, 6m, 18d.
Color: White
Birthplace: Bedford County, TN, 8th District
Father: .T. Sullivan
Birthplace: Rutherford County, TN
Mother: Mary Crutchfield
Birthplace: Bedford County, TN
Physician: Dr. A.E. Fuston

SWING, AUBREY DOUGLAS
Date of Funeral: Oct 18, 1927   2 p.m.
Casket: Oct White, size 2/0 & Box $35.00
Date of Death: Oct 18, 1927 at Shelbyville, TN
Place of Funeral: Powell Grave Yard
Clergyman: Bro. J.E(?). C. Vanse
Interred: Powell Grave Yard
Date of Birth: Sep 11, 1927
Age: 1m, 7d.
Color: White

Birthplace: Bedford County, TN
Father: Thurman Swing
Birthplace: Bedford County, TN
Mother: Addie Caldwell
Birthplace: Bedford County, TN
Physician: Not Any

TEMPLE, MRS. MARGARET SARAH
Date of Funeral: Dec 30, 1929   1 p.m.
Casket: State Gray, plush, ½ Couch &
Hearse, Services $ 275.00
Outside Case: Cedar   40.00
Burial Garment: Gray Silk Dress   30.00
Metal Box Covers   6.00
Grave Lining   3.00
Drayage etc.   5.00
Total: $ 359.00
Date of Death: Dec 29, 1929 at Home of G.M. Comstock, in the 21st District
Place of Funeral: Home of G.M. Comstock, 21st District, Bedford County, TN
Clergyman: Rev. W.C. Creasman & Rev. Frank Jackson
Interred: Willow Mount Cemetery, Shelbyville, TN
Date of Birth: Nov 8, 1849
Age: 80y, 1m, 21d.
Color: White – Occupation: At Home
Widow
Birthplace: Bedford County, TN
Husband: Dallas Temple
Father: Murdici (?) Coleman
Birthplace: Bedford County, TN
Mother: Sarah Elizabeth Coleman
Birthplace: TN
Physician: Jas. L. Morton

THOMAS, JAMES MADISON
Date of Funeral: Mar 28, 1928   11 a.m.
Underwear, Sox $ 4.00
Casket: Sil Gray, plush, size 6/3   210.00
Box, Hearse Services   6.00
Total: $210.00
Date of Death: Mar 27, 1928 at 23rd District, Bedford County, TN
Clergyman: Rev. S.A. Jones
Interred: Burns Cemetery
Date of Birth: May 9, 1840
Age: 87 y, 10m, 18d.
Color: White – Occupation: Farmer
Widower
Father: Unknown
Mother: Unknown
Birthplace: Bedford County, TN
Physician: Rev. A.E Fuston

THOMPSON, (Infant of J.W. Thompson)
Date of Funeral: (no date given)
Casket: Sq, White, size 1/6 $ 4.00
Ambulance   2.00
Total: $ 6.00
Date of Death: Mar 17, 18-928 at Bedford County Hospital
Interred: Willow Mount Cemetery, Shelbyville, TN
Age: 0
Color: White
Birthplace: Bedford County, TN
Father: Jno. Thompson
Birthplace: Alabama
Mother: Jessie Tracy
Birthplace: Alabama
Physician: Dr. W.H. Avery

THOMPSON, HENRY SAMUEL
Date of Funeral: Dec 20, 1928   2 p.m.
Embalming $ 20.00
Casket: Chatt State Gray, size 6/3 &
Hearse, Services, Tent, Drayage, Chairs, &
Grave Lining, Sexton   325.00
Metal Vault, Style, Clark   125.00
Burial Garment: Suit, Collar, Tie, Shirt   30.00
Total: $500.00
Date of Death: Dec 19, 1928 at Home, 7th District, Bedford County, TN
Place of Funeral: Home, 7th District, Bedford County, TN
Clergyman: Rev. C.M. Piskler (?)
Interred: Sanders Grave Yard
Date of Birth: Jul 11, 1880
Age: 48y, 3m, 8d.
Color: White -- Occupation: Farmer
Married
Birthplace: Bedford County, TN
Father: Thomas Thompson
 Birthplace: Bedford County, TN
Mother: Caldonia Sanders
Birthplace; Bedford County, TN
Physician: Dr. T.R. Ray

THOMPSON, JAME EDWARD
Date of Funeral: Jan 9, 1927
Casket: Sil Gray, E.Crape, size 5/9 &
Box, Hearse, Metal Covers, Services, Suit $ 115.00
Ordered by Horace and Chas. Thompson

Date of Death: Jan 8, 1927 at 9th District, Bedford County, TN
Place of Funeral: 9th District, Bedford County, TN, Church
Interred: Houston Grave Yard
Date of Birth: Oct 18, 1896
Age: 30y, 2m, 21d.
Color: White – Occupation: Farmer
Married
Birthplace: Bedford County, N
Father: A.P. Thompson
Birthplace: Bedford County, TN
Mother: Maggie Russ
Birthplace: Bedford County, TN
Physician: Dr. A.N. Gordon

THOMPSPN, JOHN, JR.
Date of Funeral: Oct 1, 1925   3 p.m.
Casket: White, plush, size 3/0 &
Box, Metal Covers, Services $ 35.00
Ordered by Jno. Thompson
Date of Death: Sep 30, 1925 at Shelbyville, TN
Place of Funeral: Shelbyville, TN
Interred: Willow Mount Cemetery, Shelbyville, TN
Date of Birth: Sep 1, 1924
Age: 3m.
Color: White
Birthplace: Shelbyville, TN
Father: John Thompson
Birthplace: TN
Mother: Viola Vaughn
Birthplace: TN
Physician: Dr. Ray

THOMPSON, MRS. CYNTHIA
Date of Funeral: Oct 9, 1929   12:30 p.m.
Removing Remains from Depot to Willow Mount Cemetery, Shelbyville, TN $ 15.00
Metal Box Covers $ 6.00
Grave Lining   1.00
Drayage, etc   1.50
Total: $ 23.50
Ordered by Clifton Smith
Date of Death: Oct 7, 1929 at Central Hospital, Nashville, TN
Clergyman: Dr. J.S. Sibley
Interred: Willow Mount Cemetery, Shelbyville, TN
Date of Birth: ____
Age: 92 yrs.

Color: White – Occupation: At Home

THOMPSON, NRS, EMMA CARY
Daye of Funeral: Jul 20, 1927

Embalming	$ 20.00
Casket: Sil Gray, ½ couch, size 6/3 &	
Hearse, Services	450.00
Metal Vault, Style, Clark	125.00
Burial Garment: White Silk Dress	33.00
Slippers	4.00
Grave Lining	3.00
Total	$ 635.50

Ordered by H.J. Thompson
Date of Death: Jul 18, 1927 at Home, Shelbyville, TN
Place of Funeral: Shelbyville, TN
Clergyman: Dr. W.P. Powell & Dr. S.P. White
Interred: Willow Mount Cemetery, Shelbyville, TN
Date of Birth: Dec 10, 1875
Age: 51y, 7m, 8d.
Married
Color: White – Occupation: Housewife
Birthplace: Bedford County, TN
Husband: Henry J. Thompson
Father: Dr. Jno. Clary
Birthplace: North Carolina
Mother: Mattie Ogilvie
Birthplace: Bedford County, TN
Physician: Dr. T.J. Coble & Dr. Ben . Burdett

THOMPSON, MRS. T. LEIGH

Date of Funeral: Aug 10, 1927	11:30 a.m.	
Removing Remains		$ 20.00
Grave Lining		3.50
Truck for Flowers & Vault		3.00
Total:		$ 29.00

Date of Death: Aug 8, 1927 at Home, Nashville, TN
Place of Funeral: Willow Mount Cemetery, Shelbyville. TN
Clergyman: Dr. Holt & Dr. Sibley
Interred: Willow Mount Cemetery, Shelbyville, TN
Date of Birth: Nov 6, 1870
Age: 57 yrs.
Color: White – Occupation: Housewife
Married
Last place of Residence, Nashville, TN
Husband: T. Leigh Thompson

Father: Jesse Ely
Birthplace: TN
Mother: Mary Whiteside
Birthplace: Bedford County, TN
Physician: Dr. S.S. Crockett

THOMPSON, ROBERT K.
Date of Funeral: Jul 25, 1929   3:30 p.m.
Casket: Sq. Flat Top, Gray, size 6/3 &
Box and Hearse $ 50.00
Date of Death: Jul 25, 1929 at Shelbyville, TN
Place of Funeral: Shelbyville, TN
Clergyman: Rev. Keathley
Interred: Willow Mount Cemetery, Shelbyville, TN
Date of Birth: Unknown
Age: About 75 yrs.
Color: White – Occupation: Retired Laborer
Widower
Birthplace: Bedford County, TN
Father: Unknown
Mother: Unknown
Physician: Dr. Jas. L. Morton

TITTSWORTH, MRS. LUCY
Date of Funeral: Apr 13, 1929   10:30 a.m.
Casket: Oct Gray, plush, size 6/3 &
Hearse, Box, Embalming, Services $ 225.00
Date of Death: Apr 12 1928 at Lewisburg, TN
Place of Funeral: Lewisburg, TN
Clergyman: Bro. Isom
Interred: Algood, TN
Date of Birth: Jan 30, 1889
Age: 39y, 2m, 13d.
Color: White – Occupation: Housewife
Married
Birthplace: Putnam County, TN
Last place of Residence: Lewisburg, TN
Husband: U.L. Tittsworth
Father: W.L. Wright
Birthplace: Putnam County, TN
Mother: Julia Phillips
Birthplace: Putnam County, TN
Physician: Foster & Wheat

TRACY, GEO. WASHINGTON
Date of Funeral: Feb 22, 1929
Casket: Flat Top. Size 2/0 & Box $ 10.00
Date of Death: Feb 22, 1929 at Shelbyville Mills
Place of Funeral: Shelbyville Mills
Interred: Shelbyville Mills
Date of Birth: Feb 22, 1929
Age: ¼ day
Color: White
Birthplace: Bedford County, TN
Father: Robert Tracy
Birthplace: Missouri
Other: Gurtha Hale
Birthplace: TN
Physician: Dr. W.H, Avery

TRIBBLE, EARNEST JOE
Date of Funeral: Jul 9, 1928   2 p.m.
Embalming: $ 20.00
Casket: Oct Gray, size 6/3 &
Box, Hearse, Services   125.00
Metal Box Covers   6.00
Hose, Underwear   2.25
Total: $153.25
Ordered by his wife.
Date of Death: Jul 8, 1928 at 24th District, Bedford County, TN (Home)
Place of Funeral: Singleton
Clergyman: Bro. J.W. Cherry
Interred: Pisgah
Date of Birth: Jun 13, 1881
Age: White – Occupation: Farmer
Married
Birthplace: Bedford County, TN
Father: Alonzo Tribble
Birthplace: Bedford County, TN
Mother: Fanny Anthony
Birthplace: Lawrence County, TN
Physician: Dr. J.T. Conditt

TRIBBLE, MRS. NANNIE ODLE
Date of Funeral: Jan 20, 1929   12 N
Casket: Oct Gray, size 5/4 &
Box, Metals, Hearse, Services $ 95.00
Ordered by C.R. Tribble, Bell Buckle, TN, R3.
Date of Death: Home, 5th District, Bedford County, TN

Place of Funeral: Burns
Date of Birth: Unknown
Age: about 80 yrs.
Color: White – Occupation: At Home
Married
Birthplace: Rutherford County, TN
Last place of Residence: Bedford County, TN
Husband: C.R. Tribble
Father: jerry Odle
Birthplace: Unknown
Mother: Unknown
Physician: Dr. A.F. Gordon

TROXLER, JAMES HUFFMAN
Date of Funeral: Jun 2, 1925   10 a.m.
Casket: White, L.S., size 2/0 &
Box, Service, Metal Boards $50.00
Ordered by A.F. Mullins & J.M. Mullins
Date of Death: Jun 1, 1925 at Bedford County Hospital
Place of Funeral: Home of E. Huffman
Clergyman: Dr. Robinson
Interred: Jenkins Burial Ground
No other information

TUCKER, MRS. LETTIE BARTLETT
Date of Funeral: Jul 18, 1926   4 p.m.
Casket: B.C. Coffin, size 6/3 &
Box, Hearse, Services $ 65.00
Burial Garment: Dress, Hose   12.50
Metal Boards   5.00
Driver   1.00
Total: $ 83.50
Ordered by Neal Bartlett & Charged to Bartlett Bros.
Date of Death: Jul 18, 1926 at Home, Shelbyville, TN
Clergyman: Dr. S.P. White
Interred: Willow Mount Cemetery, Shelbyville, TN
Date of Birth: Don't Know
Age: About 23 yrs.
Color: White – Occupation: Pencil Factory Laborer
Widow
Birthplace: Bedford County, TN
Father: Will Bartlett
Birthplace: TN
Mother: Fannie Malone
Birthplace: TN

Physician: Dr. Bias

TURNER, JAMES FRANKLIN
Date of Funeral: Nov 1, 1928	2:30 p.m.	
Embalming		$ 20.00
Casket: State Sol., Walnut, size 6/3 &		
Hearse, Services		280.00
Outside Case: Cedar		40.00
Burial Garment: Suit, Collar, Shirt, Tie		30.00
Underwear, Sox		2.00
Metal Box Covers		6.00
Grave Lining		6.00
Drayage, etc		3.00
Total:		$389.00

Date of Death: Oct 31, 1928 at Home, Shelbyville, TN
Place of Funeral: Methodist Church, Shelbyville, TN
Clergyman: Rev. J.W. Cherry & Rev. W.E. Doss
Interred: Willow Mount Cemetery, Shelbyville, TN
Date of Birth: Aug 20, 1845
Age: 83y, 2m, 11d.
Color: White – Occupation: Retired Merchant
Married
Birthplace: Shelbyville, Bedford County, TN
Father: Monroe Turner
Birthplace: Virginia
Mother: Mary Clark
Birthplace: Bedford County, TN
Physician: Dr. Jas. L. Morton

VANDERGRIFF, MRS. MARY ELIZABETH
Date of Funeral: Sep 30, 1928   2 p.m.
Casket: Oct Gray, E. rape, size 6/3 &
Box, Hearse, Services $ 125.00
Metal Box Covers   6.00
Grave Lining   6.00
Total $ 137.00
Date of Death: Sep 29, 1928 at Home, Shelbyville, TN
Place of Funeral: Home, Shelbyville, TN
Clergyman: Rev. laude Levion (?) & Bro. Keathley
Interred: Willow Mount Cemetery, Shelbyville, TN
Date of Birth: Feb 11, 1899
Age: 29y, 7m, 18d.
Color: White: Occupation: Housewife
Married
Birthplace: Rutherford County, TN
Last place of Residence: Bedford County, TN
Husband: Robert .D. Vandergriff
Father: Tom J. Brown
Birthplace: Rutherford County, TN
Mother: Katie Newberry
Birthplace: Kentucky
Physician: Dr. A.E. Fuston

VANN, AVERY LEVOY
Date of Funeral: Jan 24, 1929   2 p.m.
Casket: Flat Top L.S., size 3/0 &
Box, Hearse, Services $ 35.00
Date of Death: Jan 2, 1929 at Home, Shelbyville, TN
Place of Funeral: Mt. Herman
Clergyman: Rev. Jess Hart
Interred: Mt. Herman Cemetery
Date of Birth: Jun 29, 1927
Age: 1y, 6m, 26d.
Color: White
Father: J.D. Vann
Birthplace: Madison County, Alabama
Mother: Ethel Wilhoit
Birthplace: Bedford County, N
Physician: Dr. W.H. Avery

VAUGHN, ELISHA
Date of Funeral: Oct 6, 1925   2p.m.
Embalming $ 15.00
Casket: Blk E. Crape, size 6/3 &

Box, Hearse, Services	$ 100.00
Blk. B.C. Robe	15.00
Metal Box Covers	5.00
Total:	$ 135.00

Date of Death: Oct 4, 1925 at Shelbyville, TN
Place of Funeral: Residence at Shelbyville, TN
Clergyman: Dr. Robinson
Interred: Willow Mount Cemetery, Shelbyville, TN
Date of Birth: Feb 12, 1853
Age: 72 yrs.
Color: White – Occupation: Carpenter
Married
Birthplace: North Carolina
Last place of Residence: Shelbyville, TN
Physician: Dr. Ray

VAUGHN, MRS. CALLIE
Date of Funeral: Sep 17, 1929   2 p.m.

Embalming	$ 20.00
Casket: Blk E. Crape, size 6/3x &Box, Hearse, Services	100.00
Metal Box Covers	6.00
Grave Lining	3.00
Total:	$ 129.00

Date of Death: Sep 15, 1929 at Home, Olie Watson, Shelbyville, TN
Place of Funeral: Home, Olie Watson, Shelbyville, TN
Clergyman: Dr. Julian Sibley
Interred: Willow Mount Cemetery, Shelbyville, TN
Date of Birth: ____
Age: 73y, 1m, 29d.
Widow
Birthplace: Bedford County, TN
No other information

VERNON, JAMES McFADDEN
Date of Funeral: May 25, 1926   3 p.m.

Embalming	$ 20.00
Casket: Sil Gray, plush, size 6/3 &	
Oval Cap, Box, Hearse, Services	200.00
Burial Garment: Suit	30.00
Underwear, Sox	1.50
Metal Boards	5.00
Grave Lining	2.00
Total:	$ 285.50

Date of Death: May 24, 1926 at Home, Shelbyville, TN
Place of Funeral: Home, Shelbyville, TN

Date of Birth: Sep 7, 1852
Age: 73 yrs.
Married
Birthplace: Shelbyville, Bedford County, TN
Father: Wm. T. Vernon
Birthplace: TN
Mother: Martha Lawrence
Physician: Dr. J.L. Morton

VERNON, MRS. TENNIE
Date of Funeral: Sep 10, 1928   3 p.m.
Embalming $ 20.00
Casket: Oct Sil. Gray, plush, Oval Top, Hinge Cap, size 6/3 &
Box, Hearse, Services   200.00
Metal Box Covers   6.00
Grave Lining   6.00
Total: $232.00
Date of Death: Sep 9, 1928 at Home, Shelbyville, TN
Place of Funeral: Home, Shelbyville, TN
Clergyman: Rev. Frank Tinder
Interred: Willow Mount Cemetery, Shelbyville, TN
Date of Birth: Feb 18, 1855
Age: 73y, 6m, 21d.
Color: White – Occupation: Housewife
Widow
Husband: J.M. Vernon
Physician: Dr. Jas. L. Morton

VICK, MARY ETTA
Date of Funeral: Jan 29, 1927   10:30 a.m.
Casket: Sq. Flat Top, Crape, size 5/4 &
Box, Hearse, Metal, Services $ 25.00
Date of Death: Jan 28, 1927 at Home, Dayton Row
Place of Funeral: Home, Dayton Row
Clergyman: Dr. J.L. Vanse
Interred: Willow Mount Cemetery, Shelbyville, TN
Date of Birth: Mar 29, 1906
Age: 20 yrs.
Color: White
Single
Birthplace: TN
Father: Sam Vick
Birthplace: TX
Mother: Mary Stevson
Birthplace: Alabama

WALKER, WILLIAM C.
Date of Funeral: Apr 7, 1927   2 p.m.
Casket: Blk E. Crape size 5/9 &
Hearse, Services, Box, Metals, Robe $ 125.00
Date of Death: Apr 7, 1927 at Home of F.R. Bearden
Place of Funeral: Home of F.R. Bearden
Clergyman: Dr. J.E. Vanse
Interred: Willow Mount Cemetery, Shelbyville, TN
Date of Birth: May 20, 1850
Age: 76y, 10m, 8 d.
Color White – Occupation: Farmer
Married
Birthplace: Bedford County, TN
Father: Caloway Walker
Birthplace: Unknown
Mother: Unknown
Physician: Dr. T.R. Ray

WALLACE, JAMES ANDREW
Date of Funeral: Dec 23, 1928   10:30 a.m.
Removing Remains from Home &
Embalming, Dressing etc $275.00
Casket: Oct Gray, plush, size 6/3 & Box &
Suit, Underwear, Sox, Hearse, &
Lining, Franklin, T., $10.00 pd.
Total: $275.00
Date of Death: Feb 22, 1928 at Home, 7th District, Bedford County, TN
Place of Funeral: M.E. Church, TN
Clergyman: Rev. J.W. Cherry
Interred: Franklin, TN
Date of Birth: Jul 9, 1861
Age: 66y, 7m, 13d.
Color: White – Occupation: Farmer
Married
Birthplace: Williamson County, TN
Last place of Residence: Bedford County, TN
Father: Jas. H. Wallace
Birthplace: TN
Mother: Rebecca Jones
Birthplace: Williamson County, TN
Physician: Dr. T.J. Coble

WALLING, MRS. DELLA EULESS
Date of Funeral: Jun 1, 1927   4:30 p.m.
Dressing, etc., Silk Hose, &

Casket: Gray, State, size 6/3 &
Grave Lining, Dress, Clark Vault, Hearse, Service $ 650.00
Date of Death: May 30, 1927 at Home, Shelbyville, TN
Place of Funeral: Home, Shelbyville, TN
Clergyman: Dr. Chas. Armstrong
Interred: Willow Mount Cemetery, TN
Date of Birth: Oct 10, 1864
Age: 62y, 7m, 20d.
Color: White – Occupation: Housewife
Married
Birthplace: Shelbyville, Bedford County, TN
Husband: Jet Walling
Father: Martin Euless
Birthplace: Bedford County, TN
Mother: Cassie Bobo
Birthplace: Bedford County, TN
Physician: Dr. Ben L. Burdett

WARD, JOHN WESLEY
Date of Funeral: Jun 21, 1925

Removing Remains	$ 6.00
Embalming	25.00
Burial Garment: Gents B.C. Suit	25.00
Underwear, Sox	2.00
Total:	$ 58.00

No other information.

WARNER, MRS. ANNIE ELIZABETH
Date of Funeral: Feb 12, 1927   2 p.m.

Embalming	$ 20.00
Casket: White L.S., size 6/3 &	
Box, Hearse, Services	125.00
Burial Garment	33.00
Slippers	3.00
Flowers	16.00
Metal Box Covers	6.00
Grave Lining	xxx
Total:	$197.00

Ordered by Mr. and Mrs. Jno. W. Herron
Date of Death: Feb 9, 1927 at Bedford County Hospital, Shelbyville, TN
Place of Funeral: Home of Jno. W. Herron
Clergyman: Rev. Kelly
Interred: Willow Mount Cemetery, Shelbyville, TN
Date of Birth: Aug 31, 1909
Age: 17 yrs.

Color: White – Occupation: Pencil Factory Hand
Married
Birthplace: Wilson County, TN
Last place of Residence: Shelbyville, TN for 17 years
Husband: Geo. Warren
Father: Jno. W. Herron
Birthplace: TN
Mother: Hattie Barrett
Birthplace: Wilson County, TN
Physician: Dr. W.H. Avery

WARNER, MRS. EMMA R.
Date of Funeral: Nov 28, 1928   2 p.m.
Hearse,(2 trips & Personal Service $ 100.00
Metal Vault, Style lark (illegible Copper)   450.00
Box Mattress   3.00
Grave Lining   12.00
Drayage, Tent, Chairs & etc   12.00
(Cemetery Bill $27.00)   Total: $ 578.00
Date of Death: Nov 10, 1928 at Pasadena, California
Place of Funeral: Baptist Church, Shelbyville, TN
Clergyman: Rev. Claude Davis & Rev. Creasman
Interred: Willow Mount Cemetery, Shelbyville, TN
Date of Birth: Apr 14, 1842
Age: 86y, 6m, 26d.
Color: White – Occupation: Housewife
Widow
Birthplace: Kentucky
Last place of Residence: California
Husband: Thomas W. Warner
Father: Wm. Trail
Birthplace: TN
Mother: Eliz Jane H(illegible)
Birthplace: Kentucky
Physician: Warren F. Fox

WARREN, MRS. ALICE
Date of Funeral: Jun 29, 1925   2 p.m.
Casket: Sil Gray, E. Crape, size 5/9 $ 125.00
Metal Box Covers   5.00
Crape D. Dress   25.00
Pr. Silk Hose   1.50
Total: $ 156,50
Ordered by Alvis Warren
Date of Death: Jun 28, 1925 at 22nd District, Bedford County, TN

Place of Funeral: Raby Grave Yard
Clergyman: Rev. Jesse Hart
Interred: Raby Cemetery, (Moore County, TN)
Date of Birth: ____
Age: ____ - Occupation: Housewife
Married
Birthplace: TN
Husband: Alvis Warren
Physician: Dr. Conditt

WARREN, MRS. MINNIE GORE
Date of Funeral: Mar 21, 1927   2 p.m.
Casket: Sil Gray, E. Crape, size 6/3 &
Box, Hearse, Services $ 125.00
Burial Garment   25.00
Metal Box Covers   6.00
Total: $ 156.00
Ordered by Chas. Warren
Date of Death: Mar 20, 1927 at Home, 22nd District, Bedford County, TN
Clergyman: Rev. Jesse Hart
Interred: Pleasant Garden Cemetery
Date of Birth: Jan 22, 1892
Age: 36y, 1m, 26d.
Color: White – Occupation: Housewife
Birthplace: Bedford County, TN
Husband: Chas. Warren
Father: Wiley Gore
Birthplace: Moore County, TN
Mother: Victoria Patterson
Birthplace: Bedford County, TN
Physician: Dr. J.T. Coble

WATKINS, MRS. PINK
Date of Funeral: May 17, 1929   11 a.m.
Casket: B. & Box, size 6/3 $ 35.00
Ordered by E. Cobb
Date of Death: May 16, 1929 at Home, 22nd District, Bedford County, TN
Interred: New Herman Cemetery
Date of Birth: Feb 2, 1876
Age: 53y, 3m, 16d.
Color: White – Occupation: At Home
Married
Birthplace: Bedford County, TN
Husband: General Watkins
Father: Pierce Willhoit

Place of Birth: Bedford County, TN
Mother: Eliza Jane Wilhoit
Birthplace: Bedford County, TN
Physician: Dr. Conditt

WATSON, CARNEY HOWARD
Date of Funeral: Oct 8, 1926   3 p.m.
Embalming $ 20.00
Casket: Sil Gray, E. Crape, size 6/3 &
Box, Hearse, Services   125.00
Burial Garment: Suit Cloths, Collar, Tie, Shirt   28.00
Metal Box Covers   6.00
Grave Lining   2.00
Total: $ 181.00
Ordered by Olie Watson
Date of Death: Oct 6, 1926 at Home, Shelbyville, TN
Place of Funeral: Home, Shelbyville, TN
Clergyman: Dr. J.E. Vanse
Interred: Willow Mount Cemetery, Shelbyville, TN
Date of Birth: Feb 15, 1909
Age: 17y, 7m, 21d.
Color: White – Occupation: Harness Maker
Single
Birthplace: Bedford County, TN
Father: Olie Watson
Birthplace: TN
Mother: Martha Vaughn
Birthplace: TN
Physician: Dr. J.L. Morton

WELSH, JAMES MARTIN
Date of Funeral: Mar 27, 1929   2 p.m.
Casket: Oct Gray, L.S., size 3/0 &
Box, Hearse, Services Metals $ 38.00
Date of Death: Mar 26, 1929 at Home, Shelbyville Mills
Place of Funeral: Shelbyville Mills
Interred: Cotton Mills Grave Yard
Date of Birth: Nov 26, 1927
Age: 1y, 4m.
Color: White
Birthplace: Bedford County, TN
Father: Mark welsh
Birthplace: Bedford County, TN
Mother: Argie May Cunningham
Birthplace: Bedford County, TN

Physician: Dr. Jas. L. Morton

WHEELER, JOHN DESKIN
Date of Funeral: Oct 1, 1925   1:30 p.m.
Casket: Blk B.C., size 6/3 &
Box, B.C. Suit, Hearse, Services $ 170.00
Ordered by W.O. & H.T. Wheeler
Date of Death: Sep 30, 1925 at 8th District, Bedford County, TN
Place of Funeral: Hickory Hill Church
Clergyman: Bro. Agee & Ben Norman
Interred: Wheeler Grave Yard
Date of Birth: May 8, 1848
Age: 77 yrs.
Color: White – Occupation: Farmer
Widower
Birthplace: TN
Last place of Residence: 8th District, Bedford County, TN
Physician: J.L. Morton

WHEELER, MRS. NANNIE
Date of Funeral: Feb 13, 1927   2 p.m.
Casket: Oct Gray, E. Crape, size 5/9 &
Box, Hearse, Services, Robe $ 100.00
Ordered by Elisha Wheeler
Date of Death: Feb 12, 1927 at Bedford County Hospital
Place of Funeral: North Fork Church
Clergyman: Dr. Agee & Kerney
Interred: Pressgrove Grave Yard
Date of Birth: Jan 5, 1885
Age: 42y, 1m, 7d.
Married
Birthplace: Bedford County, TN
Husband: Elisha Wheeler
Father: Joseph M. Orr
Birthplace: Bedford County, TN
Mother: Margaret Jane Anderson
Birthplace: Bedford County, TN
Physician: Dr. W.H. Avery

WHEELER, WILLIAM NORRIS
Date of Funeral: Feb 17, 1928   10 a.m.
Embalming $ 20.00
Casket: Gray crape, size 6/3 &
Box, Hearse, Services   100.00
Burial Garment: Suit   14.00

Metal Box Covers $ 6.00
Total: $ 140.00
Ordered by Oscar Wheeler
Date of Death: Feb 16, 1928 at Home of Oscar Wheeler
Place of Funeral: M.E. Church, Shelbyville, TN
Clergyman: rev. J.W. Cherry
Interred: Wheeler Grave Yard
Date of Birth: Oct 3, 11900
Age: 27y, 4m, 13d.
Color: White – Occupation: Shipping Clerk
Married
Birthplace: Bedford County, TN
Father: Oscar Wheeler
Birthplace: Bedford County, TN
Mother: Ellen Landers
Birthplace: Bedford County, TN
Physician: Dr. T.R. Ray

WHITTMORE, GEORGE DAVID
Date of Funeral: Aug 9, 1929   11 a.m.
Casket: White L.S., size 3/6 &
Box, Hearse, Metal Boards $ 59.00
Date of Death: Aug 8, 1929 at Home, 6th District, Bedford County, TN
Place of Funeral: Harts Chapel
Clergyman: Rev. Keathley
Interred: Harts Chapel
Date of Birth: Oct 11, 1925
Age: 3y, 9m, 27d.
Color: White
Father: Willie Whittmore
Birthplace: Bedford County, TN
Mother: Catherine Reed
Birthplace: Bedford County, TN
Physician: Dr. Jas. L. Morton

WIGGINS, JOHN DAVID
Date of Funeral: Apr 21, 1926   2 p.m.
Removing Remains from Train to home of Fred Wiggins $ 15.00
Metal Box Covers   5.00
Total $ 20.00
Date of Death: Apr 18, 1926 at Denver, Colorado
Place of Funeral New Hermon
Clergyman: Dr. Watson
Interred: New Hermon
Date of Birth: May 11, 1901

Age: 25 yrs.
Color: White
Married
No other information

WIGGINS, MRS. ANNIE LEE
Date of Funeral: Sep 28, 1924   3 p.m.
Embalming $ 15.00
Casket: White, plush, ½ couch, size 6/0   225.00
Total: $ 240.00
1 Doz. Chairs (no charge)
Metal Grave Cover (no charge)
Date of Death: Sep 27, 1924 at Shelbyville, TN
Place of Funeral: Lynchburg, TN
Clergyman: Watson & Beason(?)
Interred: Lynchburg Cemetery
Date of Birth: Nov 1, 1886
Age: 37 yrs.
Color: White
Married
Birthplace: ____
Husband: C.W. Wiggins
Father: J.H. Jones
Mother: ____
Physician: Dr. T.R. Ray
Cause of Death: Nephentis (?)

WILHOIT, MRS. FINETTA
Date of Funeral: Jun 10, 1927   2:30 p.m.
Casket: Flat Top, Gray rape, size 6/3 $ 75.00
Burial Garment: Comforter   12.50
Total: $ 87.50
Ordered by Andrew Wilhoit
Date of Death: Jun 9, 1927 at Home, Shelbyville, TN
Place of Funeral: Naz. Church, Mt. Herman
Clergyman: Rev. S.A. Jones
Interred: Mt. Herman Cemetery
Date of Birth: Mar 2, 1868
Age: 58y, 3m, 6d.
Color: White – Occupation: Housewife
Married
Birthplace: Moore County, TN
Last place of Residence: Shelbyville, TN
Husband: Andrew Wilhoit
Father: Daniel Thompson

Birthplace: Unknown
Mother: Unknown
Physician: Dr. W.H. Avery

WILHOIT, MRS. MARTHA & TWO INFANTS
Date of Funeral: Aug 19, 1926   10:30 a.m.
Removing Remains from Wartrace to Shelbyville, TN &
From House to Cemetery $ 20.00
Metal Box Covers   6.00
Grave Lining   2.00
Total: $ 28.00
Ordered by Jim Wilhoit
Date of Death: Aug 16, 1926 at Toledo, Ohio
Place of Funeral: Shelbyville, TN
Clergyman: Dr. J.C. Robinson
Interred: Willow Mount Cemetery, Shelbyville, TN
(Two infants (girl)
1 Premature Births, Aug 16, 1926)
Date of Births: ____
Age: 18 yrs.
Married
Last place of Residence: Toledo, Ohio
Husband: Jim Wilhoit
Father: ____
Other: Mrs. ____ Thompson

WILHOIT, SARAH (COL)
Date of Funeral: Mar 321, 1928   2:30 p.m.
Casket: Blk E. Crape, size 6/0 & Box $ 90.00
Burial Garment: Blk Robe   5.00
Metal Box Corvers   5.00
Total: $100.00
Ordered by Lovie Wilhoit
Date of Death: Mar 30, 1928 at Shelbyville, TN
Clergyman: R.L. Dowell
Date of Birth: ____
Age: ____
Color: Colored)
Physician: Dr. Watson

WILHOITT. JOHN
Date of Funeral: Mar 24, 1926   2 p.m.
Casket: White, plush, size 3/0 &
Box, Hearse, Services $ 35.00
Ordered by Jim Wilhoitt

Date of Death: Mar 23, 1926 at Home, near Jenkins Chapel
Place of Funeral: Mt. Herman
Clergyman: Rev. Jess Hart
Interred: Herman Cemetery
Date of Birth: Apr 3, 1924
Age: 2 yrs.
Color: White
Physician: Dr. W.H. Avery

WILLIAMS, CHAS. GREGORY
Date of Funeral: Mar 31, 1926   10 a.m.
Casket: Gray Vel., size 6/3x &
Box, Hearse, Metals, Services, Embalming $400.00
Silk Comforter   8.00
Metal Box Covers   5.00
Total: $413.00
Date of Death: Mar 29, 1926 at 24th District, Bedford County, TN
Place of Funeral: Home, 24th District, Bedford County, T
Interred: Flat Creek
Date of Birth: Jan 2, 1870
Age: 56 yrs.
Color: White – Occupation: Farmer
Married
Birthplace: Bedford County, TN
Father: Francis Williams
Birthplace: TN
Mother: Mat Stegall
Birthplace: TN
Physician: Dr. J.T. Conditt

WILLIAMS, AMES ESTLE
Date of Funeral: Sep 20, 1929   10 a.m.
Casket: Oct plush (old stock) &
Box, Hearse, Metals, Services $ 25.00
Date of Death: Sep 19, 1929 at Home, Shelbyville, TN
Place of Funeral: Home, Shelbyville, TN
Clergyman: Rev. W. Creasman
Interred: Houston Grave Yard
Date of Birth: White
Age: 3m, 11d.
Color: White
Birthplace: Rutherford County, TN
Father: Joe E. Williams
Birthplace: Bedford County, TN
Mother: Onella (Omella?) Lynch

Birthplace: Wilson County, TN
Physician: Jas. L. Morton

WILLLIAMS, JOHN A.
Date of Funeral: May 16, 1925   10 a.m.
Embalming $ 20.00
Underwear, Sox   5.00
Casket: Blk B.C. size 6/3 &
Box, Extra Trio with Hearse   10.00
Burial Garment: Gents Robe   15.00
Slippers, Night Sheet   1.50
Total: $ 226.50
Ordered by Pink Mullins
Date of Death: May 15, 1925 at Hospital, Shelbyville, TN
Place of Funeral: Flat Creek, TN
Clergyman: Bro. Geo. Gowan
Interred: Flat Creek Cemetery
Date of Birth: May 8, 1859
Age: 66 yrs.
Color: White – Occupation: Farmer
Physician: Dr. Conditt

WILLIAMS, MRS. SOPHRONIA
Date of Funeral: Jun 214, 1925   2 p.m.
Embalming $ 20.00
Casket: Sil plush, size 6/3 &
Box, Hearse, Services   200.00
Metal Box Covers   5.00
Total: $ 225.00
Ordered by Mannon Mullins
Date of Death: Jun 13, 1925 at 22nd District, Bedford County, TN
Place of Funeral: Flat Creek
Clergyman: Rev. Hart
Interred: Flat Creek Cemetery
Date of Birth: Oct 9, 1847
Age: 78yrs.
Color: White
Widow
Physician: Dr. Conditt

WILLIAMS, MRS. TENNIE DAVIS
Date of Funeral: Nov 30, 1928
Casket: Elliptic Belmont, Gray, plush, size 6/3 &
Box, Hearse, Services $ 265.00
Metal Box Covers   6.00

Drayage, Tent, & etc. $ 10.00
Total: 281.00
Date of Death: Nov 29, 1928 at Home, 22nd District, Bedford County, TN
Place of Funeral: New Herman, TN
Interred: New Herman Cemetery
Date of Birth: Sep 27, 1862
Age: 66y, 2m, 2d.
Color: White – Occupation: Housewife
Married
Birthplace: Bedford County, TN
Father: John Davis
Mother: Rhoda Dixon
Physician: Dr. Conditt

WINFORD, JAMES FLOYD
Date of Funeral: Jan 30, 1928   2 p.m.
Casket: Oct Gray, E. Crape, size 6/3 &
Box, Hearse, Services, Shirt, Tie $ 127.50
Date of Death: Jan 29, 1928 at Home of C.A. Leonard, 3rd District, Bedford Co., TN
Plače of Funeral: Church of Christ, Shelbyville, TN
Clergyman: Bro. E.P. Watson
Interred: Willow Mount Cemetery, Shelbyville, TN
Date of Birth: July 8, 1901
Age: 26y, 6m, 26d.
Color: White – Occupation: Auto Mechanic
Divorced
Birthplace: Lincoln County, TN
Last place of Residence: Bedford County, TN
Father: Ben Winford
Birthplace: Franklin County, TN
Mother: Ophelia Pigg
Birthplace: Lincoln County, TN
Physician: Dr. J.P. Taylor

WINSETT, JOHN EARNEST
Date of Funeral: Mar 20, 1929   11 a.m.
Casket: Oct Cleveland size 6/3 &
Box, Hearse, Robe, Services $ 90.00
Date of Death: Mar 19, 1929 at Home, 7th District, Bedford County, TN
Place of Funeral: Home, 7th District, Bedford County, TN
Clergyman: Rev. R.L. Stem
Interred: Robinson Yard
Date of Birth: May 2, 1901
Age: 27y, 10m, 17d.
Color: White – (afflected)

Single
Birthplace: Rutherford County, TN
Last place of Residence: Bedford County, TN
Father: John T. Winsett
Birthplace: Rutherford County, TN
Mother: Arrie Heath
Birthplace: Rutherford County, TN
Physician: Dr. W.H. Avery

WISEMAN. MRS. SALLIE

Date of Funeral: Sep 24, 1926	11 a.m.	
Casket: Blk E. Crape, size 5/9 &		
Box, Hearse, Services		$100.00
Metal Box Covers		6.00
Total:		$106.00

Date of Death: Sep 23, 1926 at Home, Shelbyville, TN
Place of Funeral: Ross (Raus)
Date of Burial: Sep 24, 1926
Interred: Bomar Grave Yard
Date of Birth: Jan 13, 1842
Age: 84y, 8m, 10d.
Color: White – Occupation: Housewife
Widow
Birthplace: Bedford County, TN
Physician: Dr. T.R. Ray

WOMACK, JOHN HARMON

Date of Funeral: Apr 2, 1929	2 p.m.	
Casket: Oct Gray, plush, size 6/3 &		
Hearse, Services & etc		$ 280.00
Metal Vault, Style: Clark		125.00
Burial Garment: Shirt, Suit , Collar, Tie		31.00
(Flowers: $30.00) Pd.	Total:	$ 436.00

Date of Death: Apr 1, 1929 at Home, Shelbyville, TN
Place of Funeral: Lynchburg, TN (Moore Mounty, TN)
Clergyman: Rev. Coleman
Interred: Lynchburg, TN
Date of Birth: Jul 13, 1859
Age: 69y, 8m, 18d.
Married
Birthplace: Moore County, TN
Last place of Residence: Bedford County, TN
Father: Frank Womack
Birthplace: Moore, County, TN
Mother: Mildred Green

Birthplace: Moore County, TN

WOMACK, WALTER EMMET
Date of Funeral: Sep 0, 1927   4:30 p.m.
Casket: White, L.S., size 4/6 &
Box, Hearse, Services $ 35.00
Ordered by Mill Relief Fund
Date of Death: Sep 10, 1917 at Home, Shelbyville, TN
Place of Funeral: Parker Grave Yard
Clergyman: Not Any
Interred: Parker Grave Yard
Date of Birth: Jun 6, 1921
Age: 6y, 3m, 4d.
Birthplace: Warren County, TN
Father: J. Wommack
Birthplace: Warren County, TN
Mother: Lockie Webster
Birthplace: Bedford County, TN
Physician: Dr. W.H. Avery

WOOD, WILLIAM (COL)
Date of Funeral: Nov 13, 1928   1 p.m.
Casket: Gray, Robe, Hearse, Services $ 50.00
Date of Death: Nov 9, 1928 at Nashville, General Hospital
Place of Funeral: Colored Cemetery, Shelbyville, TN
Interred: Colored Cemetery, Shelbyville, TN
Date of Birth: ____
Age: 51 yrs.
Color: Colored – Occupation: Laborer
Married
No other information

WOODS, CORNELIA WHITHERSPOON
Date of Funeral: Oct 20, 1927   4:30 p.m.
Removing Remains from Tullahoma, TN to Shelbyville, TN &
Services $ 25.00
Special Gray Lenin   7.85
Drivers, Drayage & etc   3.50
Total: $ 36.35
Cemetery: $6.00.
Date of Death: Oct 19, 1927 at Wesley Long(?) Hospital, at Greensboro, NC
Clergyman: Dr. Julian Sibley
Interred: Willow Mount Cemetery, Shelbyville, TN
Date of Birth: ____
Age: 8m, 29d.

Birthplace: Greensboro, North Carolina
Last place of Residence, Greensboro, North Carolina
Father: J. Albert Woods
Birthplace: Bedford County, TN
Mother: Cornelia Whitherspoon
Birthplace: TN
Physician: Russell O. (illegible), Greensboro, North Carolina

WOODS, GEORGE ALBERT
Date pf Funeral: Mar 20, 1927   3 p.m.
Embalming $ 20.00
Casket: State Steel, size 6/3 &
Hearse, Personal Service   325.00
Outside Case, Cedar   30.00
Grave Lining   3.00
Metal Box Covers   6.00
Drayage & etc.   5.00
Total: $ 389.00
Ordered by J.A. Woods
Date of Death: Home, Shelbyville, TN
Place of Funeral: Presbyterian Church, Shelbyville, TN
Clergyman: Dr. James S. Vance & Dr. J.W. Cherry
Interred: Willow Mount Cemetery, Shelbyville, TN
Date of Birth: Apr 11 (No year given)
Age: 59y, 11m, 8d.
Color: White – Occupation: Banker
Married
Birthplace: Bedford County, TN
Father: Geo. B. Woods
Birthplace: TN
Mother: Margaret Clark
Birthplace: TN
Physician: Dr. T.J. Coble

WOODS, JAMES ALLEN
Date of Funeral: Mar 6, 1929   2:30 p.m.
Embalming $ 20.00
Casket: Chatt 1010 Gray, size 6/3 &
Hearse, Service   325.00
Outside Case, Cedar   35.00
Underwear, Shirt, Collar, Tie, Sox   5 .00
Grave Lining   6.00
Metal Box Covers   6.00
Drayage for Box, Chairs, Flowers, etc.   4.50
Total: $ 401.50

Date of Death: Mar 5, 1929 at Home, Shelbyville, TN
Place of Funeral: Presbyterian Church, Shelbyville, TN
Clergyman: Dr. J.S. Sibley
Interred: Willow Mount Cemetery, Shelbyville, TN
Date of Birth: Nov 10, 1861
Age: 67y, 3m, 23d.
Color: White: Occupation: Retired Traveling Salesman
Married
Birthplace: Bedford County, TN
Father: George Woods
Birthplace: TN
Mother: Margaret Clark
Birthplace: TN
Physician: Dr. T.R. Ray

WOODS, MRS. FANNIE SANDUSKY

Date of Funeral: Oct 6, 1927	3 p.m.	
Embalming		$ 20.00
Casket: 1010 Gray, size 6/3 &		
Hearse, Services		325.00
Outside Case, Cedar		30.00
Metal Box Covers		6.00
Grave Lining		3.00
Drayage, Drivers, & etc		9.50
Total:		$393.50

Ordered by Cecil & Albert Woods
Date of Death: Oct 5, 1927   2 p.m.
Place of Death: Home, Shelbyville, TN
Place of Funeral: Home, Shelbyville, TN
Clergyman: Dr. J.S. Sibley & Dr. J.W. Avery
Interred: Willow Mount Cemetery, Shelbyville, TN
Date of Birth: Dec 15, 1870
Age: 56y, 9m, 22d.
Color: White – Occupation: Housewife
Widow
Birthplace: Bedford County, TN
Husband: G. Albert Woods
Father: Dr. G.C. Sandusky
Birthplace: Kentucky
Mother: Ellen Rodgers
Birthplace: TN
Physician: Dr. T.J. Coble

WOODWARD, GERMON
Date of Funeral: Jan 1, 1927
Embalming $ 20.00
Casket: Gray Plush, size 6/3 &
Box, Hearse, Services, Underwear   200.00
Metal Box Covers   5.00
Total: $225.00
Date of Death: Jan 10, 1927 at Home, 20th District, Bedford County, TN
Place of Funeral: Home, 20th District, Bedford County, TN
Interred: Richmond, TN
Date of Birth: Sep 6, 1846
Age: 80y, 4m, 4d.
Widower
Birthplace: Bedford County, TN
Father: Germon Woodward
Birthplace: Virginia
Mother: Margaret Dolason (?)
Physician: Dr. W.H. Avery

WOODWARD, JOHN BURTON
Date of Funeral: May 6, 1927   11 a.m.
Dressing, etc, $ 10.00
Casket: Oct plush, size 6/3 &
Hearse, Services   200.00
Outside Case, Cedar   35.00
Metal Box Covers   6.00
Grave Lining   3.00
Total: $254.00
Ordered by Mrs. Jno. B. Woodward
Date of Funeral: May 5, 1927 at Home, 20th District, Bedford County, TN
Place of Funeral: Big Spring Baptist Church
Clergyman: Dr. Taylor
Interred: Willow Mount Cemetery, Shelbyville, TN
Date of Birth: May 27, 1893
Age: 33y, 11m, 7d.
Color: White – Occupation: Farmer
Married
Birthplace: Bedford County, TN
Father: Arch P. Woodward
Birthplace: Bedford County, TN
Mother: Mary Eva Foster
Birthplace: Marshall County, TN
Physician: Not Any
Cause of Death: Suicide (shot gun)

WOOSLEY, JNO. (DICK) MILTON
Date of Funeral: Jan 6, 1926   10 a.m.

Removing Remains from Hospital	$ 3.00
Embalming	20.00
Casket: Gray B,C, 6260, size 6/3 &	
Box, Hearse, Services	325.00
Burial Garment: Suit, Collar, Tie	35.00
Underwear, Sox	2.50
Grave Lining	2.00
Metal Box Covers	5.00
Ambulance	3.00
Total:	$395.50

Ordered by H.L. Woosley
Date of Death: Jan 5, 1926 at Hospital, Shelbyville, TN
Place of Funeral: Shelbyville, TN
Clergyman: Dr. J.N. Cherry & Dr. S.P. White
Interred: Shelbyville, TN
Date of Birth: Sep 20, 1867
Age: 58yrs.
Color: White – Occupation: Lumberman
Single
Physician: Dr. T,J. Coble

WOOSLEY, MRS. ELIZABETH
Date of Funeral: Feb 5, 1925

Embalming	$ 10.00
Casket: Gray B.C., ½ couch	325.00
Metal Vault, Style, Clark	125.00
Total:	$460.00

Date of Death: Feb 4, 1925 at Bedford County, TN
Place of Funeral: Home
Clergyman: Watson
Interred: New Hope Cemetery
Date of Birth: Jul 8, 1846
Age: 78yrs
Physician: Dr. T.R. Ray
No other information

WOOSLEY, MRS. LIZZIE
Date of Funeral: Dec 4, 1928   2 p.m.

Embalming	$ 20.00
Casket: Oct White, size 6/3 &	
Box, Hearse, Personal Service	125.00
Burial Garment: Silk Dress, Hose	19.00
Metal Box Covers	6.00

Total: $ 170.00
Date of Death: Dec 3, 1928 at Shelbyville Mills, Bedford County, TN
Place of Funeral: Home, Shelbyville Mills, Bedford County, TN
Clergyman: rev. Frank Tinder
Interred: Holland Grave Yard
Date of Birth: Apr 12, 1879
Age: 49y, 7m, 21d.
Color: White – Occupation: Housewife
Widow
Birthplace: Bedford County, TN
Father: C.M. Adcock
Birthplace: Lincoln County, TN
Mother: Fanny Womack
Birthplace: TN
Physician: Dr. W.H. Avery

WORD, MRS. MARTHA JOSEPHINE
Date of Funeral: Jun 1, 1928   4 p.m.
Embalming $ 20.00
Casket: Oct , B.. Cedar, size 6/3 Nat.   250.00
Outside Case Cedar   35.00
Burial Garment: white Silk Winding Sheet   18.00
Metal Box Covers   6.00
Grave Lining   6.00
Total: $ 335.00
Ordered by Mrs. Edna Anderson
Date of Death: May 31, 1928 at Home, Shelbyville, TN
Place of Funeral: Methodist Church, Shelbyville, TN
Clergyman: Rev. J.W. Cherry & Rev. Chas. H. Armstrong
Interred: Willow Mount Cemetery, Shelbyville, TN
Date of Birth: Nov 7, 1850
Age: 77y, 6m, 23d.
Color: White – Occupation: Housewife
Widow
Birthplace: Bedford County, TN
Father: Nimrod Burrow
Birthplace: North Carolina
Mother: Sallie Ann Landis
Birthplace: Bedford County, TN
Physician: Dr. T.J. Coble

WRIGHT, ROBERT SYLVESTER
Date of Funeral: Jan 14, 1928   1 p.m.
Casket: Oak Black, size 6/3 &
Hearse, Services $ 100.00

Outside Case, Cedar	$ 30.00
Burial Garment: Suit	15.00
Metal Box Covers	6.00
Total:	$ 151.00

Ordered by R. (?). Parsons
Date of Death: Jan 13, 1928 at Home, 8th District, Bedford County,
Place of Funeral: Crowells Chapel
Clergyman: Bro. R.L. Stem
Interred: Crowells Chapel Cemetery
Date of Birth: Mar 14, 1880
Age: 47y, 9m, 29d.
Color: White – Occupation: Merchant
Single
Birthplace: Bedford County, TN
Father: Clemont H. Wright
Birthplace: Bedford County, TN
Mother: Rhoda Jane Smotherman
Birthplace: Rutherford County, TN
Physician: Dr. W.H. Avery

YANCY, CLAUDE H.

Date of Funeral: Aug 27, 1926 2 p.m.	
Embalming	$ 20.00
Casket: Sil Gray, State, size 6/3 &	
Hearse, Services	325.00
Outside Case: Cedar	25.00
Burial Garment: Suit (Gray), Shirt, Collar, Tie	28.00
Metal Box Covers	6.00
Grave Lining	2.00
Underwear	1.50
Total:	$ 407.50

Ordered by Wife
Date of Death: Aug 26, 1926 at Home of Wm. Dixon, 3rd District of Bedford County, TN
Place of Funeral: Jenkins Chapel
Clergyman: Dr. Chas. Armstrong
Interred: Jenkins Chapel Cemetery
Date of Birth: Aug 19, 1926
Age: 40y, 7d.
Color: White – Occupation: Farmer
Married
Birthplace: Bedford County, TN
Father: William H. Yancy
Birthplace: TN
Mother: Rebecca Shoffner
Birthplace: TN
Physician: Dr. T.J. Coble
Cause of Death: Self-inflicted gun shot wound

YANCY, MRS. ELLA

Date of Funeral: Nov 23, 1924 3 p.m.	
Embalming	$ 15.00
Casket: Gray, size 6/(3?)	120.00
Metal Vault, Style, Clark	125.00
Total:	$260.00

Ordered by Frank Yancy
Date of Death: Nov 22, 1924 at Shelbyville, TN
Place of Funeral: Shelbyville, TN
Clergyman: S.P. White
Interred: Willow Mount Cemetery, Shelbyville, TN
Date of Birth: Apr 3, 1881
Age: ____
Color: White – Occupation: Housewife
Married
Birthplace: Shelbyville, TN

Husband: Frank Yancy

YOUNG, GEO. WASHINGTON
Date of Funeral: Apr 7, 1926   11 a.m.
Casket: Gray Crape, size 6/3 &
Box, Hearse, Services $ 125.00
Burial Garment: Suit   30.00
Underwear, Sox   1.50
Metal Box Covers   5.00
Total: $ 161.50
Date of Death: Apr 6, 1926 at Home, Shelbyville, TN
Place of Funeral: Home, Shelbyville, TN
Clergyman: Dr. White
Interred: Willow Mount Cemetery, Shelbyville, TN
Date of Birth: Nov 1, 1882
Age: 34 yrs.
Color: White – Occupation: Printer
Married
Birthplace: Don't Know
Last place of Residence: Shelbyville, TN
Physician: Dr. W.H. Avery

YOUNG, MRS. LUA (?) CUMMINGS
Date of Funeral: In Chicago, Feb 7, 1926
Removing Remains from Train to Cemetery $15.00
Metal Vault, Style, Clark   125.00
Total: $140.00
Ordered by Miss Mabel Robson(?)
Date of Death: Feb 6, 1926 at Chicago, Illinois
Place of Funeral: Chicago, Illinois
Date of Birth: Feb 9, 1926
Interred: Willow Mount Cemetery, Shelbyville, TN
Date of Birth: ____
Age: 72y, 7m, 22 d

www.ingramcontent.com/pod-product-compliance
Lightning Source LLC
Chambersburg PA
CBHW020458030426
42337CB00011B/144